Praise for
Welcome Home

We all love stories of miracles: the sick get well and the lame walk—it's done! Healed! Over! God showed up as God. But what about stories of triumph—stories where the healing doesn't take place instantly, but God shows up moment by moment, day after day? We don't always get the miracle we pray for, but we can have God's strength and wisdom to triumph one day at a time.

Kim's grandparents—Ray and Dot Frappier—and their children were with my husband, Jack, and me from the beginning of Precept Ministries International, where we learned to discover God's Word and truth inductively. This book is a testimony of triumph that comes when you know God and His Word firsthand. In the Woodhouse story, the next generation shows how to live out truth, how to live "normally" in a difficult place. You'll love it, and you'll learn by example how to find joy. Isn't that one of the Divine byproducts of trials?

—KAY ARTHUR, best-selling author and cofounder and co-Chief
Executive Officer of Precept Ministries International

Kimberley Woodhouse's frank and warm narrative about her family's rocky journey to extreme joy is a book to be reread and treasured, but make sure you have a tissue handy. I loved this book, and it was such an encouragement to me when I was dealing with my beloved father-in-law's advancing Alzheimer's. A book for the keeper shelf!

—COLLEEN COBLE, best-se'''
of the Rock Harbor serie

Here's a story packed with encouragement and evidence of God's graciousness. Whatever your problems and pressures, the Woodhouse story will encourage you to keep trusting Him—and keep on keeping on.

—DON HAWKINS, DMin, President of Southeastern Bible College

My impression of *Welcome Home: Our Family's Journey to Extreme Joy* is exactly the same as my impression of this incredible woman who wrote their family story: amazing! Through their trials they (as the saying goes) became better, not bitter. They chose joy and have inspired me to look at the bumps along my own road as opportunities to rise and fly instead of moan and groan.

—DONITA K. PAUL, best-selling author
of the DragonKeeper Chronicles

I not only recommend this story of hope, but I am privileged to call the Woodhouse family our friends. Kim could have focused on the sorrow and pain of family events, but instead she writes about God's tenderness and mercy. Throughout their journey, this family could have chosen to quit—to give up, but they kept on going with the joy of the Lord as their strength. This book is for those who desire that same joy and hope for themselves.

—TRACIE PETERSON, best-selling author of over 80 books
including The Brides of Gallatin County series

Welcome Home presents a beautiful portrayal of a mother's love transcending all obstacles. Kim's words inspire us all to recall what really is important along this journey. I've had the pleasure of spending the day with the Woodhouse family—but if you can't, read this beautiful book and relish in the joy of coming home.

—GARY WRIGHT, Southern Living At Home

Welcome Home!

OUR FAMILY'S JOURNEY TO EXTREME JOY

Kimberley Woodhouse

Tyndale House Publishers, Inc.
CAROL STREAM, ILLINOIS

Editor: Marianne Hering
Designed by Ron Kaufmann.
Cover photographs of family, teddy bear, packing the cooler, and swimming taken by Stephen Vosloo, copyright © by Tyndale House Publishers, Inc. All rights reserved.
Cover photograph of Kayla looking out the window by Todd Reeves, copyright © 1998 by *El Dorado News Times*. All rights reserved. Used with permission.
Cover photograph of Kayla sitting by a machine copyright © by Kimberley Woodhouse. All rights reserved.

The author is represented by the literary agency of Alive Communications Inc., 7680 Goddard Street, Suite 200, Colorado Springs, CO 80920, www.alivecommunications.com.

Library of Congress Cataloging-in-Publication Data
Woodhouse, Kimberley, 1973-
 Welcome home : our family's journey to extreme joy / Kimberley Woodhouse.
  p. cm.
 "A Focus on the Family book."
 Includes bibliographical references.
 ISBN 978-1-58997-573-6
 1. Sensory disorders in children. I. Title.
 RJ496.S44W66 2009
 618.92'8—dc22
                                    2009016451
ISBN-13: 978-1-58997-573-6

Printed in the United States of America
1 2 3 4 5 6 7 8 9 / 15 14 13 12 11 10 09

Dedicated to

Jeremy, Josh, and Kayla—

I love you with all my heart.

You inspire me each and every day on this adventurous road we call life,

and you help me define my very own normal.

Contents

Foreword by David Phelps ix

Acknowledgments xiii

Introduction 1

1 "If Something's Going to Happen, It's Going
   to Happen to Kim" 7

2 "I Want Answers—and I Want Them Right Now!" 27

3 Fearfully and Wonderfully Made 49

4 Trial by Fire 61

5 Alaska? Are You Serious? 75

6 Isolated Island Joy 93

7 Sliding Downhill 103

8 Joy in the Darkness 123

9 When the World Falls Apart . . . Don't Quit 141

10 The Brain Is an Amazing Thing 157

11 That Famous Megaphone Announcement 177

12 That's What Love Is 199

Resources 218

Notes 219

Foreword

My band and I were on the last leg of my first solo tour of the West Coast. We made our way from Tennessee to Amarillo, Texas, and then to Santa Fe, New Mexico. From there, we went to California and up the coast. After a few shows we began to make our way back home: Nevada, Utah, and then to Colorado. We had had some very memorable concerts, but one stuck out: Colorado Springs. It was an interesting night altogether. We were in a smaller venue than normal, and as a result, it was difficult for our production crew to load in and set up as they had planned. I was excited about Colorado Springs because I had only been there a couple of times. The city was a growing market for me, and that interested me a lot. But though the crowd was more than enthusiastic, it turned out to be a little smaller than anticipated. There were also some sound problems, and my voice was tired. Not one of my better nights.

After the concert I made my nightly trek to the merchandise table to shake hands with fans and take photos. After I signed the first few autographs, I talked with a young couple who had worked their way up to the front of the line. The guy said, "We just have to know . . . Why are you here?"

I paused for a moment, realizing that this would take more than a simple "Thank you."

"What do you mean?" I asked.

He went on, "Well, this is a really small place, and none of the other tours come here. They all come to the bigger hall on the other side of town." Before I could speak, he added, "We just think you should be in the bigger venue."

I smiled, knowing that this was a compliment, but also to cover up my disappointment that we couldn't even fill the smaller venue. "Thank you, but this is where God led us this time. We weren't able to schedule that hall when we could be here. Maybe next time we'll have better luck."

The couple smiled and expressed how much they enjoyed the evening, and then I moved on to the next person in line. I was tired, depressed, ready to go back to the bus. The line moved on. I was doing my best to spend a fair amount of time with each person and to be kind to those waiting.

"Thank you."

"Sure I'll sign it."

"Do you want me to make it out to someone?"

Why am I here? Why weren't there more people here? I hope no one was disappointed.

I don't remember her walking up. Actually, I must have still been thinking about the bigger venue because my memory of the encounter begins after she was into her story. I was concerned that she was taking too long with her story and that those behind her would become frustrated. But as I focused on her, something inside of me said, *Stop. Listen. This is why you're here.*

I remember I set my Sharpie down and relaxed against the table. The story unfolded. The room disappeared. It was a moment bigger than my agenda. I was caught up in it. I couldn't help but memorize her face. Tears. Anxiety. Joy.

The story, as you will read, was of her daughter, Kayla, a huge fan with a terrible burden—or was it a blessing? Her joy confused me. There were tears in my eyes and in hers. I struggled to keep up with her story, and before I could react, she was saying good-bye and rushing out the door. I looked into the eyes of the next person in line.

After a moment I said, "Will you wait one moment, please?" I turned to my assistant and quickly got his attention. "Please go after her and find out how I can contact her."

That night in the front lounge of the bus, I told everyone the story of Kayla and the Woodhouse family, about her life-threatening condition, and about the miraculous hope on the horizon. The night was a success. Had I been in the bigger venue, it might have all passed me by.

An amazing journey started for me that evening. Phone calls, letters, television shows. A relationship started that will last long after this body gives out.

Rewind five years . . . or was it six? The details are blurry. It was a hectic time. I was in a large arena that evening. The tour had been long, and one city often looked like the last. After a long night on stage and then meeting fans, I was making my way to the bus when I felt a hand on my shoulder. I turned to see a woman in her early 60s. Out of breath, she gasped, "I've been trying to find you in here before they close the doors." She caught her breath and then went on. "My granddaughter introduced me to your music. She was a huge fan of yours. She would stand in her room . . . *(tears began)* in her hospital room and sing 'End of the Beginning,' 'My Child Is Coming Home,' and 'Virtuoso.' " The woman placed a photograph in my hand of a beautiful little girl singing to a teddy bear she was lifting in the air.

"She wanted so badly to meet you, but we weren't able to catch you last time you were here. She died of leukemia this year."

I was stunned.

"I want you to have this photo and to ask you one thing: please don't forget her."

I managed to whisper, "I won't."

In my home office, in my right-hand desk drawer, there rests a photo of a beautiful little girl. Each time I open that drawer, I fulfill my promise. I lift up the photo and speak to it: "Sweetheart, I have not forgotten."

But I don't remember her name. I missed the chance to learn from her struggle, to experience her joy. I missed a chance to know victory. I missed a chance to see God. I was in the bigger venue.

I tell you all this not to pull at your heartstrings but because I simply desire to reinforce the experience you are about to have as you read the story Kim has painstakingly journaled. As you traverse its lines, let it encourage you to rest in the small venues of your life. The Glory . . . the Light of Life, I have learned, is in those moments.

Reaching out to Kayla has not commandeered my life. It has not depleted my time, emotions, or energy. It has not infringed upon my space. It has expanded the boundaries of my world, my influence, and my joy.

Listen to the soul stories around you in the seemingly insignificant moments. Take in the depth of their emotion and make their loss, their pain, and their victories your own. Use this chronicle of inspiration as your catalyst to pour yourself into the thirsty lives around you. And in doing so, each of us might just be able to follow the lead of the Woodhouse clan and discover laughter from tears, joy from pain, insight from confusion, and victory from victimhood. Now that's an extreme makeover.

David Phelps
Recording Artist and Songwriter

Acknowledgments

My Lord and Savior, Jesus Christ—whose grace, love, and forgiveness give me a second chance every day. To God be the glory.

Jeremy—my husband and best friend. I love you. It hasn't been easy, but we wouldn't have grown so much. Thanks for encouraging me and sticking with me on this incredible, joy-filled journey.

Josh and Kayla—I love you both so very much. I love the time we have together, and I love being your mom. I praise God every day for giving you to me. Thank you for your hugs, your laughter, your encouragement, and your cheers of "Mom is the best author ever!" (Even if you are a little biased.) The Lord has used you both to touch so many lives—keep your focus on Him.

Mary Lombard—my sister and biggest fan. When you read the first story, you encouraged, raved, advised. Thanks for cheering me on all these years. And thanks to my brother, Ray Hogan, who has given me more stories than I could ever tell.

Garry and Judy Hogan, James and Brenda Woodhouse—Thanks for loving and supporting us through it all.

Deanna Chang—We've shared our laughter, our embarrassing situations, our grief, and our struggles. Thank you for traveling this road with me—and for hitting me over the head. I love you.

Leah Patteson, Chris Heitstuman, Janelle Jay, Erica Duval, Eryn Kahler, Trisha Carter, Jacque Nethken, Tammy Vachris—a few of my precious friends. I could write a book just about all of you. Thank you.

Holly Volstad—You were so much fun to have as a student and are even more fun now as a friend. You are so very talented, my dear. Use it all for Him. Thank you for all your help over the years.

David and Lori Phelps—Your family is so special to us. Thank you for everything. You're a living testimony to what love truly is.

Kelly M.—You know who you are. Thank you. Thank you. Thank you.

To the writers' groups WWW and His Writers—Thank you for your prayers, support, and encouragement.

Jim and Tracie Peterson—for challenging me to write, write, write. And praying with us all these years. Your friendship has blessed me beyond measure.

Donita K. Paul—Thank you for taking the time to have a "dragon" conversation with Josh, for taking us all under your wing, challenging, mentoring, and encouraging me—but most of all, for being such a special friend. I love you!

Colleen Coble—I'll never know why you chose to be my friend, but I sure do love you. Thank you for giving of yourself, mentoring me, critiquing, brainstorming, and listening. You are so very special to me.

Carrie Kintz—I never imagined that a bookstore meeting could turn into an incredible friendship. Thank you for your prayers, encouragement, and "telling it like it is." You are such a blessing to me.

Ronie Kendig—my new critique partner and blessed friend. I'm so thankful God brought us together. Thank you for your insight and hugs. You are amazing.

Heather Diane Tipton—friend, critique partner, assistant, and publicist. You wear so many hats, but I can't tell you how grateful I am to have you in my life. Thank you.

Lori Healy—You jump in and do anything and everything to make it all possible. You've been there through the TV cameras, the craziness, the endless phone calls and e-mails. I'd never make it through all the chaos without you, my friend and loving assistant.

Beth Jusino—We connected from the very beginning. Thank you for being my very own "agent extraordinaire," caring about my family and me, not just my books and career. You are amazing.

Matt and Shannon Swanson—You guys are so special. Thank you. Thank you for opening up your hearts to us. Thank you for sacrificing so very much for our family. The treasure of your friendship has brought us so much joy.

Dr. Edgar—Thank you for putting all of the pieces of the puzzle together and diagnosing Kayla. Your words of encouragement still resonate with me today.

Drs. Margot Crossley and Stephen Smith—You are amazing doctors who have taken so much of your time to do the incredible task of helping with our day-to-day issues. Thank you for your dedication and care.

Marianne Hering—my editor on this project. Thank you so much for all of your hard work and dedication, your encouragement, and your prayers.

The teams at Focus on the Family and Tyndale Publishers—Thank you. A book is a huge project with so many different facets. I don't even know how many people were involved, but I so appreciate all of your time and efforts.

Sarah Moody—We miss you. I know you're with the Lord now, but thank you for all you did. You reached out to our family and to thousands of others, too.

To NASA—I wish I could meet each person who had a hand in developing the cooling equipment that changes our lives every day. Thank you for giving Kayla some "outside" time.

For the tens of thousands of people who have contacted me through my Web site—Thank you for caring and sharing our story with others.

And to all my readers, I pray the Lord blesses you through the journey to joy.

And lastly, to the wonderful city of Colorado Springs—The entire community helped build us a home and gave us its friendship and love. God bless you!

Introduction

Life is full of surprises.

What I thought would be a simple outing turned into an incident with a rolling ice chest, a couple of armed security agents, and what they believed might be dynamite. Yep, that's me and my normal everyday life.

This particular adventure started as my family went through a Transportation Security Administration (TSA) checkpoint at the Colorado Springs Airport. As we waited on the far side of the metal detectors and scanners for our items to roll through on the conveyor belt, the line stalled. I grabbed my shoes, coat, and camera bag and then helped the kids get their backpacks. But the conveyor belt refused to cough up the rest of our belongings. The serious, unblinking, highly trained—and did I mention *armed?*—security guards moved the rest of my fellow travelers to another scanning station.

The scanner must not be working, I thought. *Or I bet someone's in big trouble.* I casually glanced around to see who looked suspicious and capable of having illegal items in their carry-on luggage. There's a troublemaker in every bunch.

A moment later the truth hit me in the face. *I am the bad guy.* I swallowed loudly. *I am the troublemaker.*

The armed agents were concerned with one particular item. They ran it through the scanner again. And again. Finally a TSA agent walked toward me with the problem in his gloved hands. "Is this yours?"

There it was. The ice chest containing my daughter's cooling packets for her vest.

"Yes, sir," I replied, reaching to relieve him of it.

"Ma'am, don't touch the bag. We're going to have to detain you and check this out." He looked stressed. And unhappy. And he had a gun.

Everyone in the waiting area stared at me as if I wore a neon sign flashing, "Over here! Look at me!"

My ever-faithful, don't-put-me-in-the-spotlight husband took the children and found a seat. Quietly. And *away* from me. The kiddos whispered their questions to their daddy as they waited to see the outcome of Mom versus the armed men.

More agents arrived, and the "item" was swiped with some magic cloth. I pondered my situation. *This can't be good. The one in front looks like he wants to arrest me, and that one over there looks as if he wants to shoot me.*

My heart stuttered when I heard the words "possible bomb" a few times. Gulping down my impulse to try and explain, I attempted to look nonchalant. And nonsuspicious.

They were still discussing me when one TSA agent glanced at me, looked back down, and then with lightning speed, his head popped back up as his eyes grew in size and lit with recognition. "Hey, aren't you the *Extreme Makeover* lady?"

Whew! I'd never been so thankful someone recognized me from TV. They knew who I was, they knew my story, and finally they knew *why* I was carrying an ice chest onto a plane. Things made sense to them now. I was allowed to explain my unusual carry-on, and a smile slowly appeared on each of their faces as they sighed in relief.

One man walked over, shook my hand, and told me how much he loved our show. Another apologized for the delay and then advised me that on our return trip from New York City, I might want to warn airport security about the ice chest *before* it went through the scanner.

The combination of the ice chest, plugs, cords, and cooling packets—

which look similar to a certain packaging of dynamite, I'm told—made them all wonder if I was going to blow up the plane. Wow! No wonder Captain Security looked as if he was ready to take me down!

Yep, my life is full of surprises.

The doozy was finding out that my daughter has an exceptionally rare nerve disorder called hereditary sensory autonomic neuropathy (HSAN). (Try saying *that* five times fast!) Kayla doesn't sweat or feel pain, and she had brain surgery two years ago.

My family's story has been all over the newspapers, in magazines, and on national television. And during all of these appearances and interviews, there's been a common hurdle I've had to jump.

That hurdle has been the subject of normality.

Would you like to guess which question the media asks me the most? "Will Kayla ever have a chance at a normal life?"

Let me tell you right now, I'm quick to share that God made Kayla just the way she is, and she has an abundant, overflowing life ahead. But it's not like everyone else's normal.

Do you ever get tired of hearing the word *normal*? I know I sure do.

"It's just *normal* everyday life . . ."

"Can't you pick a *normal* color?"

"She looks *normal* to me."

There's even a *normal* heading choice at the top of my screen as I type this. So, obviously, Microsoft Word has some sense of normality.

What is normal, anyway? And how on earth are we supposed to achieve it? "Normal," according to the eleventh edition of *Merriam-Webster's Collegiate Dictionary*, is defined as follows:

- conforming to a type, standard, or regular pattern
- occurring naturally

- of, relating to, or characterized by average intelligence or development
- free from mental disorder

Okay, let's tackle these definitions. Do you think you conform to a type, standard, or regular pattern? I know I sure don't!

What about occurring naturally? Yes, I occurred naturally. You?

Average intelligence or development? Please, I don't know anyone who wants to be average.

Let's move on. Free from mental disorder. Hmm. Think about that one for a moment. Do we really want to address whether or not our minds are in order? Our thoughts? Mine tend to scatter on a daily basis. No comments, please.

Why do we feel this great need to fit in to a predetermined definition of normal? And why do we try to fit others into *our* normal?

Let me share with you what I've discovered in my ever-present quest to jump that mountain-sized hurdle of normality. I learned a long time ago that my life would never be anyone else's "normal," and I'm okay with that.

In the midst of everyday life, we all have complications. Some are mild, but some are so astronomically large, you begin to wonder, "How on earth am I supposed to survive this?"

In living this incredibly difficult yet inspiring journey, I have learned how to grab on to joy in every situation. Did you know that joy is not the same as happiness? Happy is in the dictionary as well as unhappy, but have you ever tried to look up unjoy? There isn't one. Why? Because even when you are sad, God's joy is still there. Even when life has you at the end of your rope, God's joy is still there. It can't be taken away. Let me put it this way—happiness is a feeling, but joy is more than a fleeting feeling;

it's the source. It's what I call my "normal-o-meter." When people ask me how I keep smiling, my answer is joy.

Now, I'm not a psychologist, a counselor, or a doctor of any kind. I'm *me*. I'm a wife and a mom. I've tried, and more often than I would like, I've failed. Miserably.

And, are you ready for this revelation? I am *not* perfect!

I am, however, perfectly normal.

Did you read that? You're probably wondering how on earth I could make that statement after examining *Webster's* definition. But hold on. In coming up with my normal-o-meter, I also had to redefine *normal*.

So here it is. *Normal* defined by Kimberley Woodhouse: "The unusual standard—it is irregularly patterned, nonaverage, occurring chaotically, and full of mental liveliness and creative flow."

You see, my house is a chilly 64 degrees year-round. You need a coat, a scarf, and woolly slippers to survive in it. All our friends have to come to our house, so they just bring their winter gear, even in July. I don't take my children many places because my daughter doesn't sweat or feel pain and has incredibly severe allergies.

It's my life, and it's my normal.

God gave you the same thing, a perfectly normal-to-you life. Stop comparing it to the lives other people live or the life other people *think* you should live and move on with what you have been given. You have your very own normal-o-meter. So jump out of the box.

Who's with me?

"If Something's Going to Happen, It's Going to Happen to Kim"

When my husband, Jeremy, and I decided we were ready to start our family, I had no idea what lay ahead on the road we were about to travel. Most young couples dream of the happily-ever-after, smooth-and-straight, follow-your-dreams road. Had I known then about all the bumps on the road, I might have quit and run away. But thankfully, I am *not* in charge, and I had to take it all one step at a time.

The first step toward parenthood took a year. After I had several miscarriages, the doctor decided to correct a minor problem through surgery. He thought this procedure would increase my chances of being able to carry a baby full term.

I was sitting on the table, ready to be put under for the surgery. The doctor told me he would be "right back." He and the nurse rushed out of the room. The whole situation had already been an emotional roller coaster for me, so I didn't handle those words with patience, or logic, for that matter. I sat there in a paper dress and thought, *I'm going to die. They found something and don't know how to break it to me. I bet I have cancer. Or maybe I'll never have children.*

I knew they were discussing whatever they just discovered, and rather than holding on to my faith, I created all sorts of horrendous diagnoses in my brain. That's one of the downfalls of being a creative person. We can't turn off the wheels in our brains, and we can imagine just about anything and be quite dramatic about the whole process.

While I contemplated how I would break the devastating news to my husband, the doctor returned, smiling. "You're not having surgery today, Kim."

"I'm not?" *Oh, boy. Here it comes. He's trying to soften the blow.*

"No. You're not. You're pregnant."

My mind ignored him as my thoughts continued their depressing track and ping-ponged around in my head. *I knew it. I need to ask how much time I have left. I need to be strong . . .*

Wait a minute . . . Did he just say pregnant?

The shock must have registered on my face because he repeated the news.

Instead of feeling excitement, I cried.

I knew I only had a 50-50 chance of carrying that child without the surgery, and so I was afraid. Afraid to get excited. Afraid I would lose another baby. Afraid to live my life with God's pure joy.

That fear almost swallowed me whole—until the nurse put her hand on my shoulder. And I saw tears in my doctor's eyes. They had been through the trenches of grief with me several times. They knew the risks. They knew the statistics. But they also knew Who was in control. They wanted to share the blessing of life with me.

In that brief moment, the first seed of hope began to take root. The doctor looked at me with kindness and reminded me where my treasures needed to be stored. The root system grew deeper, and I could feel optimism blossoming inside me.

"One day at a time," he said.

I nodded and smiled through my tears. Yes. We were going to take it one day at a time. I realized I had been holding on to my burdens, the loss of those other children. And doing that had almost drowned me in a pit of despair. So I released the grief and handed the sadness over to the Lord.

After that moment, the visit rushed by. The doctor and nurse inundated me with instructions and information. I was high risk. I would have to come back every other day to give blood. They warned me not to do much of anything active.

I got dressed and prepared to leave. With a stack of paperwork in hand, I thanked the staff and started out the door to meet Jeremy. There was a tug on my arm, and I turned to see the nurse. With tears in her eyes, she hugged me and slipped a small piece of paper into my hand. Once I had greeted Jeremy and settled in the car, I opened the note. A Bible verse: "Consider it pure joy, my brothers, whenever you face trials of many kinds, because you know that the testing of your faith develops perseverance. Perseverance must finish its work so that you may be mature and complete, not lacking anything" (James 1:2–4). The words were familiar but had never touched me like they did that day.

And the journey to joy began.

"Morning" Sickness and Dr. Pepper

During the time we were taking our first steps to becoming parents, Jeremy was taking steps in his career and had taken a new job. Just days before I found out I was pregnant, he had packed all of our belongings into a moving truck and had driven it eight hours across three states from Birmingham, Alabama, to Moss Bluff, Louisiana. He unloaded the truck into our little one-bedroom rental house and drove back to Birmingham to get me.

Six weeks later, I had lost 24 pounds. My arms were black and blue from having my blood drawn. And I definitely did *not* have the "pregnant glow."

I longed for someone—*anyone*—to say, "Oh, don't you just glow!" instead of, "Wow, are you okay? You don't look so good."

Whoever gave it the name "morning" sickness needed to hang out with me for a while. It was morning, afternoon, evening, all night, 24-hour-a-day sickness. Green was my new color.

My dear Jeremy didn't know how to help me. I hid in the bathroom with a towel over my face so he could eat and I wouldn't have to smell anything. He routinely asked me if there was anything he could do, but I was still sick. All the time.

We went on the best we could. He worried about me, and I tried not to look like death warmed over. My poor little piano and voice students knew that if I jumped up quickly, they'd better clear a path in case I didn't make it to the toilet in time. They would play easy songs like "Old Macdonald," "Twinkle, Twinkle, Little Star," or "Just as I Am" as fast and as loud as they could, because I wasn't there to correct their sloppy mistakes.

That was in some small way refreshingly comical. But my first visit to my new doctor was nothing to laugh about. He told me either the baby or I would not survive. He suggested terminating the pregnancy and even asked me whether my life was worth risking for a "fetus."

I was ticked.

He tried to convince me that my odds weren't good. But I wouldn't hear it.

"Life is not mine to give or take," I spoke through clenched teeth. "And it's not for you to decide either. That's God's job, and I'm completely offended that you would even suggest such a thing." I opened the door to leave the conference room, but I had something else to say. Looking over my shoulder at him, I spoke calmly, "And just so you understand, it's a *baby*—with a heartbeat and arms and legs, and everything else you showed me in the pictures—it's a b-a-b-y."

Then I walked out of his office.

I had no idea how to find another doctor, especially when we had no insurance. Jeremy's new job had started just days after I found out I was pregnant. The old job had great medical benefits. New job plus preexisting pregnancy equals no insurance. Oh, boy.

Jeremy didn't make a whole lot of money teaching Bible at a Christian high school, so I knew it was time to look for help. Soon after, I found a wonderful doctor—Dr. Chesterton—through a friend at church. He helped us apply for Medicaid and for a national health-assistance program for women, infants, and children called WIC. And he never once suggested taking the life of our baby. He knew the risks, he knew the statistics, and he knew where Jeremy and I stood on that issue. Because he stood in the same place.

On our second visit, Dr. Chesterton asked me how much food I had kept down. When I informed him I couldn't eat anything at all without getting sick, that wonderful man sent Jeremy to the store to buy every kind of carbonated beverage that existed. He told Jeremy there had to be *something* I could keep down that didn't have too much caffeine. Jeremy went off to search for something to help.

Dr. Pepper won the prize.

It's always been my favorite, although we never kept it in the house because it was reserved for special occasions. But when I discovered I could drink Dr. Pepper and not get sick, it became a staple. My students would bring me get-well notes and cases of soda. Forget the pickles, ice cream, nachos, and whatever else pregnant women crave. Our pantry was filled with cans of DP.

Even though I could now keep something down, I was still ill. The doctor was concerned I would deliver a premature baby, so we had to be prepared for delivery from week 20 on. Each visit the doctor would say, "Okay, let's try to make it another week." This stress seemed to make the last four months stretch into years. I swelled up like a balloon, "tossed my cookies" dozens of times a day, but I kept thinking, *One more day, one more week. Let's give this baby every chance we can.*

Jeremy taught Bible and coached basketball and baseball at the high school. He'd leave home at 6:30 in the morning, teach all day, and coach all afternoon, sometimes into the night. Traveling to out-of-district games took up even more of his time, and there were nights the team would return after midnight. My hardworking husband would call me after the last kid was picked up, and then he would head home. Despite his long work hours and resulting lack of sleep, he helped me prepare for the coming of our child. We cleaned, assembled various baby equipment "essentials," and laughed together. The bags were packed for my hospital visit, and everything was in place. And we waited.

I had begun to think Josh would never be born, and I would forever be the size of the Goodyear Blimp. (Even though I couldn't eat much at all, I was bloated by water weight.) But wouldn't you know? Josh surprised us all—my first miracle baby—and he was almost right on schedule, making his appearance March 29, 1995.

Pregnant, Again

Josh was the healthiest baby ever. (Well, of course we were biased, and the pediatrician was a little biased as well.) Roly-poly, happy, never-met-a-stranger, smiling Josh. Everywhere we went I heard, "Aww, he's soooo cute!" "You should sign him up to be a baby model!" "Look at that cute smile . . ."

Life was good. I had my wonderful (and incredibly cute) husband, my bouncing baby boy, and my fun music students. It was easy to be joyful.

And then when Josh was 15 months old, a joy-challenging trial came that would be the first of many: my grandfather collapsed in his home. We spent a lot of time on the road that summer visiting Granddaddy. It was on one of those trips that I began to feel nauseous and then sick. Really sick. Jeremy took one look at me and joked, "I've seen that face before; you must be pregnant." I didn't find it funny when I was losing my lunch, but my sweet husband was correct. I took a pregnancy test the next day, and it immediately registered positive.

The joy of a new life growing within me was, for a short time, overshadowed by grief. A few weeks later Granddaddy passed away to be with the Lord. My grandparents had been married almost 70 years. The memories and emptiness in my soul overwhelmed and devastated me.

Because of the surgery that *didn't* happen, I was in another high-risk pregnancy situation. Not long after Granddaddy's funeral, I was so drained from the pregnancy-induced illness that I couldn't even stand up. I would lie in the middle of the floor so I could at least "play" with Josh. In other words, I could still watch him as he toddled around and built things on top of me. With each passing day I became weaker. One afternoon Jeremy came home from work and found me passed out on the bathroom floor. Josh was safely napping, and we were thankful for that. But it scared us to think of what could have happened.

As Jeremy drove me to the doctor, we prayed for the tiny life inside of me and also for Josh. He didn't understand why Mommy was so sad and sick.

In the exam room Dr. Chesterton, who was grinning like a jack-o'-lantern, delivered the news that I was going to be admitted to the hospital.

Jeremy squeezed my hand for reassurance. I asked the obstetrician why he was smiling as he dished out news I didn't want to hear—I was feisty and didn't want to be confined. My pride told me I would do fine on my own, thank you very much.

He laughed at me and said, "Kim, you're not superwoman."

While I definitely understood I was *not* superwoman and most assuredly would not fit into the costume required for that job, I still didn't want to be told I needed to stay in the hospital. It simply wasn't part of my plan. And for some strange reason, I was thinking only of my own plan, not God's. It was a lesson I would have to learn the hard way.

The Hospital Disaster

So, hospital stay number one: Doctors pumped me full of fluids and medication via intravenous drip (IV). I went home. Became even sicker.

Hospital stay number two: Doctors pumped me full of fluids and medication via IV. I went home. Became even sicker.

Hospital stay number three: Doctors pumped me full of fluids and medication via IV. They made me eat red Jell-O. I told the nurse I didn't feel well. She didn't believe me. I threw up on her.

I have never been more embarrassed or upset—but she listened to me after that. I went home. Became even sicker. Though "sicker" doesn't quite seem to cover it.

Hospital stay number four: Doctors pumped me full of fluids and medication via IV. (Is anyone seeing a pattern here?) They did *not* give me red Jell-O. Instead, a stomach-settling drink they called "nausea malt" was on their list, along with some new medicine they were certain would work. Several nurses came by to see how I was doing. But the poor nurse who had to change clothes because of our prior meeting stood in the doorway, hesitant to enter. She was watching. Waiting. Worried I wouldn't make it past the first few sips.

"It's good," I told her. "I mean, it actually tastes good!"

Applause echoed all around me. I kept something down! And there was much rejoicing.

Excitement reigned in the halls that night as they put in a new IV with the miraculous medication that kept me from throwing up. I was resting comfortably, looking forward to a night without "the bucket."

Around midnight, groggy and in pain, I pressed the call button to summon the night nurse. Our conversation on the intercom went something like this:

NURSE: Yes?

ME: My arm hurts.

NURSE: Yes, ma'am.

ME (confused): My arm really hurts.

NURSE: IVs hurt, ma'am.

ME (feeling neglected): Um, I've had lots of IVs, and it's never felt like this.

NURSE: I suggest you go back to sleep, ma'am. IVs often hurt.

Click. End of conversation.

Enter Kim's temper. It's not a pretty thing, and I'm ashamed to say I was too tired to think straight. I was weak, had three IVs in me, and my arm *hurt*. I hit the call button again.

NURSE (in an agitated voice): Yes, ma'am.

ME: My arm really hurts. I can't move it. I can't bend my fingers. It's dark in here, so I can't see what's wrong with it.

NURSE: IVs often hurt.

ME: I understood you the first time you told me. But I'm trying to tell you it's hurting in an unusual way, and I need help. If you won't come look at it, would you at least send someone to turn the light on for me?

NURSE (audible huff): We change shifts in 15 minutes. You'll have to wait until the new nurse comes in.

Click. End of conversation.

At that moment I realized this poor woman considered me a pain. I didn't know what things were going on in her life to make tending her patients so distasteful, but a dehydrated pregnant woman complaining of a hurting arm did not rank high on her priority list. I felt really sorry for her and decided to pray for her.

Before I knew it, a new nurse came bouncing in. How anyone could be so energetic in the middle of the night was beyond me, but she was wonderful.

NURSE NO. 2: Do you need anything, Mrs. Woodhouse?

ME: My arm hurts. I called the other nurse, but she told me IVs often hurt.

NURSE NO. 2: Oh, my, let me turn the lights on. Is that all right?

Such courtesy.

ME: It's actually hurting worse. I'm a little worried.

NURSE NO. 2: *(Gasp!)* Oh no! (She hits a button on the wall that sends people flying into my room.)

ME: (Looking down, I see that my hand looks like a surgical glove blown up into a balloon. And my forearm is about three times the normal size.) Wow. No wonder it hurts.

NURSE NO. 2: Oh, hon, I'm so sorry we didn't take care of this earlier.

ME (giggling): It's okay. At least I'm not throwing up on anybody.

Laughter, glorious laughter was all I heard from the other nurses as they worked on my arm.

Another Reminder

Come to find out, one of my IVs wasn't in the vein it was supposed to be in. So all that wonderful fluid and medicine had filled up my arm and hand. Jeremy's words came to mind: "If something's going to happen, it's going to happen to Kim." And I laughed.

As Jeremy escorted me out of the hospital one more time, a bubbly nurse came up to me and slipped a card into my hand. The whole floor of nurses had signed their names and written notes of encouragement. The nurse who handed me the card smiled sweetly and told me they thought I needed a little pick-me-up. I read their heartfelt words and cried. Can you guess which verses were written at the bottom? James 1:2–4. Hmm. Maybe there was something I needed to learn.

The thing was, it hadn't sunk in yet.

I thought about all the wonderful people God had surrounded us with during these crazy times. No matter where we'd been, God had provided a community of encouragers, helpers, and friends. I taped the nurses' card to the fridge to remind me to count my blessings and be joyful through the tough times.

I wouldn't be able to use my right arm for more than six weeks. My poor husband, who loved my long, waist-length hair, had to help me wash it. He kept me laughing about the amount of shampoo he used compared to the "half a bottle" it took to wash mine.

I never stopped getting sick, but the new medication helped a lot. Being restricted in activity, I spent even more time in Bible study, and the book of James kept calling me.

Gasping for Life

Just before Christmas I was six months pregnant and having difficulty sleeping. I moved to the living room to read a book so I wouldn't wake

Jeremy with my tossing and turning. A loud noise was coming from Josh's room, so I waddled over to the baby monitor, mumbling under my breath, "That stinker! He's playing in his crib."

As I cranked up the volume on the monitor, I realized Josh wasn't playing—he was struggling to breathe. I raced to Josh's room, with Jeremy following on my heels. The awful croaking became faster and faster as our 21-month-old gasped for oxygen. His lips were blue, and he looked up at me in panic. His expression pleaded with me to fix it, and then exhaustion swept over him as his eyes turned glassy.

I checked his airway—nothing was stuck in there.

Time was of the essence. I picked up Josh and headed to the car while Jeremy made a dash to our room for his car keys. The reality of living a good 35 minutes from a hospital hit me hard. An ambulance would never make it out to us in time.

Gingerly climbing into our little car, I gently held Josh in my arms and strapped the seat belt around us. I tried to calm him down by rubbing his back so that maybe, just maybe, the breaths would come a little easier. The whole time I prayed, "Lord, I know he's Yours, I just wanted to have him a little longer. Take care of our little Josh, please help him be able to breathe." Tears streamed down my face as I sang and then whispered to Joshua that we loved him, and he needed to relax.

The only highway into town was under construction, and to this day, I have no idea how we got there—in *12 minutes*. Jeremy was flashing the car lights, honking the horn, and people pulled over to the shoulder to let us pass on the narrow country road. I'm convinced there were angels guiding us that night.

The emergency-room doctors were amazing. We had a panicking baby on our hands, which was making his airway constrict even more. I held him while doctors worked a mask over Josh's face and Jeremy talked to him in a soothing voice. As long as he had ahold of me and could see his daddy, Josh calmed down.

Jeremy's parents and our pastor arrived, and we stood in a circle in the ER and prayed for Josh, who was still in my arms and had an oxygen mask covering his face. The medicine took a long time to take effect, but eventually his airway opened slightly, and Josh could take shallow breaths.

The doctor in charge pulled me over to the side to tell me that Josh had acute croup. Normally, toddlers of Josh's age would be pretty sick from the croup, but it didn't tend to shut off their airways. Concern was written all over his face as he explained that Josh had been mere seconds away from needing a tube inserted in his airway. Josh would be taken to the Pediatric Intensive Care Unit (PICU), put in an oxygen tent, and monitored closely. They didn't know why his airway had shut down or why it had happened so quickly.

Another problem was my fragile pregnancy. The doctor could tell the strain of the situation had taken its toll on me. He intuitively knew I was in pain from having contractions. I hadn't thought about what I was feeling until he confronted me. As a new wave of pain washed over me, I sat down hard in the nearest chair, realizing my pregnancy was at risk.

The night was stressful, but medication and rest soon successfully stopped my contractions. I was joyful and relieved that Josh was able to breathe. As I slept on the pull-out couch in Josh's PICU room, Jeremy climbed into the oxygen tent surrounding the hospital crib and kept vigil over our little boy.

Two days later, Josh was released from the hospital. We left with gratitude and loads of medication, but no answers as to why his airway swelled shut. The doctor told us to watch him closely. At the time nothing seemed worse than hearing your child gasp for air.

I have never slept the same since.

Grocery Trip Gone Bad

The day we returned home from the hospital, I received a phone call from the billing department. The account manager patiently explained that Medicaid covered bills for the new baby and me. And while Josh had been covered for the first year, he was now almost two, and so *he was no longer covered.* No coverage for the ER. No coverage for the PICU. No coverage for oxygen tents. Ouch.

The woman who called was supernice. I could tell she didn't enjoy giving me the news about the extent of our bill, but it was her job. I was as polite as possible and willed myself not to panic. The amount we owed was half a year's salary.

After I hung up the phone, I prayed, *Lord, You know the amount of that bill. You know we don't have any extra money. Thank You for saving little Josh's life. Thank You for the hospital being willing to work with us financially. Please guide us and direct us. Give us wisdom for the coming days.*

I knew it would be hard, and I felt the peace that only He can give. And I knew we'd do our best to pay off that bill as quickly as we could.

A couple of weeks later, my blood pressure dropped, and I swelled up like a balloon—two conditions that do not usually go together. Dr. Chesterton announced that the time had finally come for me to be confined to bed rest. I protested, but he just laughed at me again.

I went by the school where my husband taught and delivered the news. I wasn't supposed to lift Josh anymore. I wasn't allowed to feed him, change his diaper, play with him—not anything. Jeremy took in the information with seriousness and asked me point-blank why I was walking around the school. Ushering me out the door, he told me not to worry; he would take care of everything. He buckled Josh into the car seat, kissed me, and sent us on our way.

Home. That's where I was supposed to go, right?

But . . . I had planned to go to the grocery store after my appointment. I had a lengthy list and knew Jeremy wouldn't have time after school, basketball practice, and the games they had that night. Plus, he had taken a second job as an interim youth pastor to help with the hospital expenses. His time was scarce. I ignored the advice of my husband and, worse, the still, small voice of God telling me to take care of myself.

Do you see where this is headed? I look back now and realize that my overorganized, list-making, itinerary-sticking personality led me right smack into the middle of trouble. I should always be on top of things, right? You know, like you're supposed to *plan* for bed rest and get all your little ducks in a row.

Just as soon as everything got done, *then* I could follow the doctor's orders. So I went grocery shopping. I know, I know, brilliant on my part. I had all kinds of excuses, like "Jeremy hasn't ever used the WIC coupons, and I don't want him to be embarrassed." But I was letting pride color my thinking. I had been uncomfortable using them, thinking people were watching me. There were times I'd wanted to scream to the masses, "My husband has a job! He works *really* hard; he just doesn't get paid much." But I have to admit that *I* am the one who cares and worries about what people think. Jeremy doesn't.

A couple of hours later, I had Josh down for a nap and was unloading all of the plastic bags when my husband called me.

"Are you all right? Where have you been?" Concern was evident in his voice.

"I'm okay."

"Where have you been?" he asked again.

"Um . . ." The thought sunk in that this hadn't been my smartest move. "At the grocery store."

Silence.

Uh-oh.

He didn't have to say anything else. All of a sudden, I didn't feel so great. I glanced down at my feet and hands and saw they were twice the size they should be. Spots danced in front of my eyes. I barely made it to the couch before I passed out.

The next thing I knew, my husband was kneeling in front of me.

"What are you doing home?" I asked. "Don't you have to coach tonight?"

He gave me that I-can't-believe-you-could-ask-such-a-thing half smile. I knew he wasn't happy with me. After a quick hug, he explained I should be taking this seriously. The doctor was serious, and he was serious. He'd already called the church and had a list of people scheduled to come stay with me every day until he got home.

A knock sounded on the door, and I knew he was serious indeed. He'd already arranged for someone to be with me that night so he could coach his varsity boys in their last big tournament. A dear, sweet friend entered, and Jeremy kissed me good-bye, told me to behave, and drove all the way back into town.

My friend stood there, hands on her hips, tapping her foot. "Kim, if you don't beat all."

I looked up at her sheepishly.

"Jeremy told me what the doctor said, and then what you attempted this afternoon. Do you need a two-by-four upside your head?"

In an instant I knew she was right. I *did* need that. How could I have been so caught up in my own plans that I was willing to risk my life and the life of the child I was carrying? Was I really that selfish? Why did I ignore God's prompting to be safe? Good grief, I've been in the ministry all my life. I'm a pastor's kid, went to Bible college, married a pastor-teacher.

I'd really like to think I knew better. Ha! Well, I just proved that theory wrong.

Today I look back fondly upon that time. It was the beginning of a new path for me. Of course, God had been trying to prepare me before this, but it took a "two-by-four moment" to truly teach me the lesson.

And let me tell you, I've had a lot of those moments since.

Flying Shoes

Bed rest was not my most favorite thing. I studied my Bible, read books, wrote letters, and watched *Veggie Tales* with Josh over and over and over again. I even finished a huge cross-stitch project. And after that? I counted all the stitches in that project: 523,612. Yep, I counted them. And that was all within the first two weeks. Only 10 more to go.

Women came to stay with me and help while I was confined to my horizontal position. Pretty soon, the biggest excitement of the day was going to the bathroom. And, yes, it was indeed something to get excited about. It was the only time I was granted the privilege of standing up, walking, and seeing a different area of the house. Wow.

The days blended together as we headed toward March. Josh was approaching his second birthday, and I was thankful he hadn't had any more croup scares. I was swollen and huge, wondering if I would ever walk normally again instead of doing that interesting waddle. Late one afternoon I received a phone call.

The precious little church where Jeremy was working as interim had taken up a love offering for our hospital bill.

Guess how much they collected?

The exact amount owed. To the very penny.

Don't try to tell me God isn't cool.

My due date approached, and one afternoon the friend who was with me for the day had to leave before Jeremy got home. I truly intended to be good, but the whole nesting thing took over, and I couldn't sit still any longer. I made my way to unload the dishwasher. I was almost done when I turned around, and there stood my husband.

If it were possible for steam to come out of someone's ears, I'm sure I would have seen some that day. I was in trouble, and I knew it. I quickly walked back over to the couch and sat down. I started rambling about how good I'd been, that it had only been this once I'd gotten up for long, and I just couldn't help myself with all these crazy pregnancy hormones.

He laughed at me, but then looked down at my feet. My ankles were so huge, my thighs could have fit inside them. Literally. Putting his serious face back on, Jeremy appeared to be choosing his words carefully. I knew I deserved a stern lecture, and so I apologized. He asked me to please not put myself at risk again, and then he finished unloading the dishwasher.

That night I had a feeling I would have the baby the next day. I told Jeremy, and he made sure everything was ready.

And wouldn't you know, around lunchtime the following day, my water broke, and I was officially in labor. Jeremy's mom, Brenda, came to stay with Josh, and Jeremy drove me to the hospital. We were so excited about this hospital—we had toured it, preregistered, and informed everyone where we would be. The overorganized, list-making personality inside of me was content.

By the time I got to the delivery room, I was in intense labor. The nurses hooked me up to the monitors, the dial needles began to sway, and green lights blinked. Suddenly Dr. Chesterton discovered a slight glitch.

Remember the surgery that never was? I needed to have that taken care of right after this new baby was born. No problem, right? Wrong. I couldn't have the surgery at that particular hospital. Why no one had thought of this before completely baffled me, but they gave me my options:

1. Have the baby at hospital A, go home, recover, have surgery six to eight weeks later at hospital B.

2. Leave hospital A in the middle of labor and go to hospital B. Have the baby and, immediately afterward, have the needed surgery.

It didn't take long for me to decide that I didn't want to recover twice with a toddler and a newborn. Jeremy agreed this was the best option, so in the midst of incredible labor, I somehow pulled my sweats back on, carried my shoes, waddled out the door, and climbed into the car.

As Jeremy pulled out of the hospital parking lot, he noted a minor problem: It was now five o'clock, and we were hitting traffic time. Oh, boy.

With Jeremy's expert maneuvering and my increasingly faster and harder contractions adding urgency, the ride to hospital B was stressful, but we were alive. Jeremy escorted me to the front door and then raced off to park the car. I waddled to the front desk and explained my situation to the attendant. But for some odd reason, she wasn't impressed with the fact I was in the last stages of labor. I told her our doctor had called ahead and was on his way.

"May I please check in and get to a delivery room?"

"Ma'am, you didn't preregister at this hospital," she answered, "so you will have to fill out the paperwork."

"Can't my husband fill out the paperwork?" I asked, breathing heavily.

"No, ma'am. *You* have to fill out the paperwork."

My sarcastic retort was cut short by a huge contraction. I threw my shoe at her desk just to make it through the pain. I could just imagine delivering a baby standing up in the lobby while I signed paperwork. I didn't realize how violent a woman in labor could be until I was in that predicament.

Thankfully, Jeremy ran through the doors at that moment and asked why on earth his wife was still standing in the lobby. The attendant tried her same little spiel on him, but he told her he wanted to see the hospital administrator right then and there.

Another contraction hit me, and I threw the other shoe, groaning through clenched teeth. Dr. Chesterton came running from the other direction and took charge. I'm thankful to say they got me into a room just in time. Kayla was born in a matter of minutes.

The rest of my hospital stay was amazing, and I'm so thankful we delivered Kayla there. And for those of you wondering, I know the woman at the front desk was just doing her job, but I must have scared her because I never found out what happened to my shoes.

CHAPTER TWO

"I Want Answers—and I Want Them Right Now!"

Kayla was a beautiful baby. She only cried when she was hungry and loved being in the middle of everything. Josh was quite the handful as a toddler, and we continually kept watch on his breathing. It felt wonderful to be up and around my own home again, and I attempted to settle into a new routine.

But something was different. I had struggled with the baby blues after Josh was born, but this time, the blahs hit me harder, and I didn't have the desire to go anywhere. I wasn't necessarily unhappy or severely depressed, but I didn't want to go to Bible study, grocery shopping, or really any place that took me out of the house. Since I'm such a social person, this struck me as odd. There were days I would sit in the rocking chair, nursing Kayla, tears streaming down my face, and ask God *why* I didn't feel like myself. What was wrong with me? I had a wonderful husband, two beautiful children, and I really *was* happy deep down—yet I still didn't want to get out.

And staying home worked well. Josh loved his baby sister. He would sit beside me on the couch and pat her head, or he would lie on the floor next to her and tell her some story that made complete sense to a two-year-old. Kayla always looked at him with adoration on her face, and I could see the bond between the two of them, even at such young ages. In fact, Josh couldn't wait for Kayla to be able to play with him. Almost every day he would ask me if it was time. Was she big enough? Could she play with him . . . finally?

One of my favorite memories is of Kayla when she was about four months old. Just as I laid her backside down on a blanket, the phone rang, and I made a mad dash to answer it. After greeting the caller, I heard Kayla giggling at her brother. This wasn't unusual, as Josh often entertained her with his silly antics. The odd part was the fact that her laughter started moving away, farther and farther down the hallway.

Throwing the phone down, I raced to see how this could possibly happen, since she hadn't even made an attempt to crawl yet. I stopped abruptly in the middle of the hall to find an unexpected sight. Covering my mouth with my hand in concern, shock, and awe, I watched as Josh dragged his little sister by the arm down the hallway. Her shoulder looked as if it had been stretched out of its socket. But Kayla giggled the whole way, while Josh kept saying, "Sissy, come pway wif me now."

I have to laugh when I look back at that scene today, but at the time, I was seriously concerned about Kayla being yanked and pulled by her arm. I talked to Josh about being more careful with his sister, but it sure was hard for my two-year-old to understand why Kayla couldn't quite play with him just yet. Kayla seemed unscathed from her excursion, but nonetheless, Jeremy and I checked her arm for days afterward.

The bond between my children grew. Josh would be ever so careful and watchful. He would entertain Kayla by playing with her baby toys, demonstrating how to use them. And as soon as Kayla learned how to crawl, she would search him out by heading straight to his room.

The months seemed to fly by, and Christmas was soon upon us. I was finally feeling more like my old self when we moved to Arkansas. Jeremy was a youth pastor and camp director, a job he had always wanted. We loved our new church and started to settle in. I was thankful the state had a wonderful program of insurance for children called ARKids First, which provided medical coverage for both Josh and Kayla. And we used it right away.

Josh had another episode where he struggled to breathe. This time, it was in the middle of the day. He had been playing when he ran to me and pulled on my leg. The distress on his face and the horrible croaking sound alerted me immediately. We raced to the hospital. The doctors were baffled that his airway would close off so quickly. Two more days in the PICU brought Josh back to normal, but I couldn't shake off the haunting sound of his gasps for air.

Heat Is a Problem

Around Kayla's first birthday, I noticed that her eczema was much worse than the infantile eczema Josh had suffered from. The new pediatrician we'd found was puzzled about the eczema's severity as well. Every day I always slathered thick creams on her skin, but the dryness and irritation kept getting worse. The doctor prescribed stronger ointments.

Up until this point, Kayla had always been the healthier one. When Josh caught the croup, Kayla never so much as wheezed. She rarely got sick, and nothing seemed to bother her. I thought that was a good thing.

In May of 1998, my perspective changed. Radically.

It all started when I decided to get out of the house for once. Since Jeremy was away at camp and we all missed him, I thought it would be a nice outing for the kiddos to visit their daddy. The weather had turned really hot—98 degrees—but we'd always lived in the South; a little bit of heat wasn't going to stop us. So I drove up to the church camp where he was the director.

I parked the van and transitioned the children out of their car seats and into the double stroller. My plan was to find my husband first, but the kids noticed a little playground a few yards away and had other ideas. Since they had been strapped in the car for more than an hour, I walked them over to the little plastic slides to play. All the while I glanced around to see if Jeremy was anywhere in sight.

Josh jabbered on in his cute three-year-old voice as I set him down and he took off running. I asked Kayla if she wanted to slide too, and she nodded. Kayla always wanted to do whatever her brother was doing. As I helped her out of the stroller, I smiled and thought about what a loving child she was, even if she was a bit of a daredevil. She could hug you so hard, it would take your breath away.

A call from Josh to watch him go down the slide brought me out of my musings. In the few seconds it took me to look over at him and back at Kayla, she was passed out on the ground, her blue eyes glazed over.

I picked her up; her body felt as if it were on fire, and her eyes slowly closed. Her skin was bright red. *Do not panic,* I told myself. *This isn't so strange. You flush scarlet when you get hot too.* As I tried to revive Kayla, Josh had caught sight of Jeremy and was waving, jumping, and hollering at him in panic. Jeremy raced over and gently took Kayla into his arms, fear and questions evident on his face.

I ran to the van, started the engine, and cranked the air-conditioning up full blast. I didn't know exactly what was wrong, but I knew my little girl was too hot. Jeremy brought her over and laid her on the passenger seat. I filled a sippy cup with cold liquid and gently poured some into her mouth, hoping the juice would trickle down her throat.

Kayla's eyes finally fluttered open to reveal more of that glassy stare, but other than that, she didn't respond to us. She was lethargic, and her skin remained a deep pink.

Jeremy and I buckled in the kids and repacked the van. Since he was responsible for a camp full of teen workers, he couldn't leave. We decided I should head back home and take Kayla to the emergency room.

Jeremy's worry was evident when he quickly kissed me good-bye. As I drove away, I looked at him again, and our eyes connected. The brief glance conveyed the entire conversation we didn't have time for: I was scared and didn't want to speed along the backwoods roads by myself. He didn't know what was wrong with our baby girl and wanted to be with us. The not-being-able-to-help was just about killing him.

About 15 minutes into the drive, Kayla started drinking voraciously. Every few minutes, Josh would pass her cup up to me and say, "Sissy thirsty, Mama." I would pull off the road and pour more juice into her cup. By the time we reached the ER, she had downed every drop of juice I had brought for the day.

Unbuckling the kids and hoisting each one on a hip, I ran inside the hospital. Kayla was still glassy-eyed and lethargic. The team went to work on her and told me her temperature was dangerously high, fluctuating between 103 and 104 degrees. They pumped her full of intravenous fluids and tried to cool her down while Josh and I looked on.

About an hour later, Kayla was sitting up and babbling like nothing had ever happened. Her temperature was coming down, and her color was returning to normal. One of the doctors came over and said the team was baffled. They weren't sure what had happened, why her temp had risen so rapidly, or why she now seemed unaffected. He said he had no choice but to discharge us and told me I should just watch her and not let her get hot. *Not let her get hot? Are you serious? But we live in the South!* Then he finished with five words I'll never forget: "The heat could kill her."

Okay, then. She won't get hot. Got it.

I wasn't thrilled with the fact that we had no answers. Only the shrugging of shoulders, a "Sorry, we can't help you anymore," and the instructions to see our pediatrician as soon as possible.

Our pediatrician was out of town, so I called from the hospital to make an appointment for the day he returned. Discouraged, and just a little worried, I wondered what to do next. I arrived home, turned the thermostat to a lower temperature, and watched my precious children play inside. I contacted the prayer chain at church and asked them to pray. Jeremy called a few minutes later, and we tried to think of a time when Kayla had been exposed to the heat before but couldn't recall one. We brainstormed on the phone for a while—something was obviously very wrong, but we had no clue what that something could be.

Later in the evening, the doorbell rang, and I opened it to find Beth Robinson, a wonderful woman from our church. She hugged me, handed me an inch-thick stack of papers, and told me she would be praying. Tears filled her eyes as she glanced at our little "sweet pea" playing on the floor. She told me she hoped the information helped and left to pick up her own child.

Beth's one of the sweetest people I know. She's a prayer warrior and such an encourager. As I watched her drive away, I glanced down at the material in my hands. Someone had done tons of research to try and help us—I found out later that it had been her husband, Jim. The very first page was from a gentleman with Cyberspace Association of U.S. Submariners (CAUSS). Jim was part of this organization as well, and these men joined together to help children who had to live in an environment like a submarine.

Upon hearing about Kayla's overheating episode, Jim knew that he and his buddies could help. CAUSS was already reaching out and helping the HED Foundation. (HED stands for hypohidrotic ectodermal dysplasia.) Children born with this disorder don't have sweat glands, so overheating is life threatening to them.

As I read through the material, it all made sense. One paragraph in particular caught my eye:

> CAUSS is a group of "online" submarine veterans who know full well the meaning of "restricted" existence. Each Dolphin Member spent many, many years within a controlled environment, living with the knowledge that invasion of that environment from the outside could very well mean death. There is an affinity for children afflicted with H.E.D. which has manifested itself into support for their *"HED Kids!"* as living memorials to their shipmates who lost their lives while serving in U.S. Submarines. They can't imagine a more suitable memorial than assisting a child with . . . *"Just Being a Kid!"* To date CAUSS has been able to fund and present Cool Vests at the rate of one each month of its existence. It is hoped that that rate will increase as its membership continues to grow.[1]

A woman named Sarah Moody had founded the HED Foundation single-handedly after rescuing her nephew who had HED. It had been a very hot day, and noting that the boy was overheating, Sarah pulled off on the side of the road, where a woman was watering her lawn. They cooled her little nephew down with the hose, saving him from a possible seizure, brain damage, and death.

In 1986, Sarah contacted NASA's Langley Research Center. She knew that if they could put a man on the moon, they could help solve her nephew's problem. With NASA's help, the cooling equipment and UV protective gear was developed, and Sarah started the foundation to help other people like her nephew.

As I read the papers Beth had left with me, little did I know that Jim and the other wonderful men from CAUSS had already contacted Sarah about a special cooling vest for Kayla.

Glad to Have Been Sad

The CAUSS information Beth and Jim provided proved to be the first step in helping baby Kayla. The second step was working with our wonderful pediatrician, Dr. Anaya, who examined Kayla two days later. He did some testing in his office and placed Kayla in a warm room. We discovered that Kayla didn't sweat; instead, she turned bright red, and her temperature jumped in a matter of minutes. Quickly placing her back in a cooler environment, Dr. Anaya expressed his concerns. HED children normally had other symptoms, such as missing teeth or very thin scalp hair. But Kayla had no other signs of the disease. He then asked me if we had ever seen her sweat. I shook my head no. That Kayla hadn't suffered severe heat stroke before this time amazed him.

That morning, my heart overflowed with thanksgiving to our great God. I thought back to all the days during my baby blues that I had asked the Lord, "Why?" I knew instantly that He had taken care of Kayla in a way I couldn't. Kayla looked perfectly healthy. There had been no signs or symptoms to warn us. And if I had felt like myself, I would have taken her to playgrounds and parks, to moms' groups and church activities. In the heat of the South, any of those situations could have killed her.

If I hadn't had postpartum depression, I probably wouldn't have Kayla with me today.

With tears streaming down my face, I told Dr. Anaya why I had kept her inside so much. And as we discussed a plan for how to control Kayla's environment, I knew in my heart we were at the beginning of a long, rough road.

A Doctor with No Answers

Dr. Anaya wasn't convinced that Kayla had HED, but he advised us to live as if she did. That meant carefully monitoring the temperature in the house and avoiding places where she might get hot. He set up appointments with a dermatology specialist at a children's hospital for a sweat test and a skin biopsy, which would determine whether HED was Kayla's diagnosis.

During the three months we waited for those appointments, we changed how we did things. Either Jeremy or I would stay with the kids while the other went to the grocery store or ran errands. The church even cooled down the nursery on Sunday mornings so that Kayla, Josh, and I could attend. Two weeks after Kayla passed out, we received a box in the mail. Someone had donated Kayla's first cooling vest. Then Sarah Moody called me with loads of information about HED. We were now recipients of the amazing technology that would change our lives.

I would be lying if I told you that this time in my life wasn't overwhelming. Some days it was easy to just ignore the obvious and keep going, and then other days my brain wouldn't stop thinking of five million different questions and "what if?" scenarios. Thankfully we had a church family who surrounded us with compassion, prayer, and support—their loving efforts kept me sane.

The teenagers from our youth group would hang out with us inside the house. They helped entertain the kiddos during these intense, hot summer months. I turned down the thermostat so the air-conditioning would blast and often fed 40 or more teens while they all crammed into the living room to watch *Veggie Tales* with Josh and Kayla. I cherish those precious memories.

A lot of those kids could have spent their summer vacations doing something else, but they chose to be with us. They understood the gravity of the situation with Kayla and wanted to help. And because they did, Josh and Kayla had more fun and more playmates than they could have ever wished for—and I had more hands and eyes to keep track of my rambunctious toddlers.

When the time finally came for our trip to the children's hospital, I just knew we would receive answers, and the doctors would be able to fix whatever was wrong with Kayla. Positive thinking, right?

After the three-hour drive, we waited in the examination room for what seemed like decades. The specialist eventually entered. He had an entourage of med students on his heels, all armed with clipboards. He asked me to start from the beginning and tell him why our pediatrician had sent us all the way up to see him. I explained briefly what had happened, and he examined Kayla's skin.

"She has eczema," he stated in a matter-of-fact manner. The entourage scribbled furiously on their clipboards.

"Yes, I know. She's had it since she was born." I was a little baffled at his lack of interest in the no-sweat issue. But still I sat on the edge of my seat, waiting to hear more, willing the answers to all our questions to ooze out of his mouth.

"She looks perfectly normal. Beautiful child." He tapped on one of the clipboards, indicating to the holder that he needed to write that down.

"Thank you, doctor."

At this point, I was totally confused. He hadn't even mentioned the tests we'd waited months for. As he patted Kayla's head and turned to whisper something to his colleagues, I quietly asked my questions. "Do you have any idea why she's overheating? Do you think she has sweat glands?"

"She has eczema." The doctor barely turned his head as he restated the fact, and then he left the room.

After the last follower left and closed the door, I looked at my husband. "Do you think he's coming back?"

Jeremy laughed. "I have no idea, but he'd better."

I married a great man. Sometimes quiet but ever watchful and fiercely protective. Normally he wanted me to handle most of the talking and asking of questions so that he could watch and pay attention to the other details. That visit was no different. But in his eyes I could see the disappointment and displeasure with the specialist growing.

Twenty minutes later, the doctor returned along with the clipboard-toting group. He examined Kayla's fingers under the light, touched her hair, asked a few questions, and then left. Again.

The next time they came in the room, the doctor immediately began talking about HED and how Kayla looked nothing like an HED patient. He was supposed to be an expert on the subject, so we listened carefully. When we showed him the vest and things from the HED Foundation, he was shocked there was such a thing. Jeremy looked at me a little oddly at this revelation. I could sense the questions burning in his mind.

The doctor continued asking questions about the foundation and the vest as the members of his group tried to notate everything. I explained that our pediatrician wasn't convinced that Kayla had HED but had requested the tests so we could get some more answers. The doctor nodded slowly, handed the vest back to me, and left the room.

I voiced the thoughts I knew both Jeremy and I were thinking. How could a doctor not know about the cooling gear for children with this condition? There were thousands of kids across the country who had been helped by the HED Foundation. I knew because I had talked to lots of their families and their doctors, and Sarah Moody had talked with almost all of them. Sarah had told us about how hundreds of other families coped and kept their children cool. She was also up on cutting-edge technology that would make more cooling gear available in the future.

The specialist returned a few more times, asking questions and touching Kayla's skin, but never once saying anything about the skin biopsies or the sweat test. After the sixth visit to our room, he left, and a few minutes later, a nurse came in with discharge papers.

Her cheery smile did nothing to settle the jumble of my insides.

"We're being sent home?" I barely squeaked the question out.

"Yes, ma'am. Your daughter has eczema." She pointed to the papers. "See? It says so, right there."

Jeremy and I exchanged a look.

My husband, who had quietly waited, watched, and listened, finally stood up. And in a tone that would brook no argument, he stated, "Please ask the doctor to come in here. Right *now*."

Now Jeremy is a no-nonsense, black-and-white, logical kind of guy—unlike me, Miss Emotional Drama Queen. The nurse didn't even bother looking to me for affirmation; she just fled the room—as fast as she could.

The doctor returned once again with his entourage. "Is there a problem?"

Jeremy was still standing, holding Kayla. He handed our toddler to me and spoke calmly yet firmly to the doctor.

"I understand that you would like to send us home with a diagnosis of eczema. But what I'm sure you don't understand is that we waited three months for an appointment with you. The instructions were simple: sweat test and skin biopsy. You did not perform either one of those tests today."

"Mr. Woodhouse—"

Jeremy held up his hand. "I'm not finished. You *did* inform us today that Kayla has eczema, a diagnosis that we already knew. You also informed us that she is beautiful and looks perfectly normal—again, facts that we previously knew. What did *not* happen today was your taking our daughter's situation seriously. It is clear that her lack of sweating and swift overheating are dangerous to her health, and yet you have offered us redundant information."

The doctor stared at us with his mouth open.

Jeremy concluded, "I have not lost respect for the medical profession today, but I have lost respect for you. And I hope *that* gets noted on all of those clipboards."

After the doctor and his group departed, the nurse gave us samples of some new creams to try on Kayla's eczema and an apology that we had to leave without the tests or a better diagnosis. We gathered up our things and left the hospital. As we drove home, I was discouraged. All this time I had been putting my hope in this one appointment, this one "expert" doctor—and I came away empty.

Crying out to God through prayer, I felt the Holy Spirit nudge my soul. I hadn't wanted to listen. I wanted things to happen in *my* timetable, according to *my* wishes. Wow. Another two-by-four moment took place that evening as I realized my only true hope was in Jesus Christ, *not* a doctor.

The next day I went with the kids to Dr. Anaya's office for a follow-up appointment. I explained what had transpired during the visit with the dermatologist. The mild-mannered pediatrician appeared more agitated as the story progressed. By the time I told him what Jeremy had said to the doctor, he was standing and pacing the room. He excused himself quickly, which left me with the sinking feeling that the news had upset him.

Thirty minutes later Dr. Anaya came back in to see us. He told me he was horrified to hear of our experience and was very disappointed the tests hadn't been performed. I knew he had a full schedule that afternoon, and we had already taken up too much of his time. We decided I should come back the next week.

Still uneasy that our kind doctor was upset, I tucked the kiddos into their car seats and drove home.

As I walked in our front door, the phone was ringing, and I scrambled to reach it before the caller hung up. Out of breath, I answered and was shocked to hear the specialist's voice from the day before. *Had Dr. Anaya called him?*

Let me say right now that I've never had anyone apologize to me like that doctor did. He sounded so humble, sincere, and totally full of remorse that he hadn't tried to help us. He explained how doctors are trained to know the answers, and he didn't want to admit in front of all his students that he did *not* have the answers in Kayla's case.

I thanked him for his phone call and apology, but before we hung up, he suggested we take Kayla to a children's hospital in a bigger city. He truly hoped we would find some answers.

Birmingham, Biopsies, and Bad News

The following week Dr. Anaya was pleased to hear about the phone call but baffled by the specialist's suggestion to try a larger children's hospital. I didn't have the heart to tell him that the dermatologist didn't want us to come back because he was embarrassed. After some deliberation, Dr.

Anaya asked us if there was another hospital we would like to try next. Since we had lived in Birmingham, Alabama, before we had kids and had a support system there, we decided it would be the best.

In September 1998 we drove to Birmingham. We spent the entire day at the hospital as doctors completed the sweat test. Kayla ran around the hospital for a couple of hours with what looked like casts on her arms for the sweat test. After that, another dermatology specialist performed the skin biopsies, which Kayla was none too thrilled about. The only thing remaining was to have a consultation with the specialist.

The doctor met us in her office and sat down with a sigh. She began by telling us the "good" news: Kayla *did* have sweat glands. But the bad news had her stumped: They couldn't make her sweat. At all. Not one drop.

The encouraging part of our discussion was learning that a lot of children grew out of their disorders by the time they were 24 months old. But if Kayla didn't grow out of it, the team at Birmingham Children's Hospital thought that would point to a neurological problem, and we would have to take her to a neurologist to determine the next step.

A Block and a Hammer

The fall was beautiful that year in Arkansas. Cooler temperatures arrived, a dear friend in our church gave us money for outdoor play equipment, and the kids loved being able to spend some time outside. Kayla wore her vest, of course, but her being outside even 20 to 30 minutes felt like a glorious gift to us all. Jeremy built me a swing in the backyard so I could sit and read or just enjoy watching the children. For a mom, there's just something sweet and special about watching your kids be kids.

My heart still yearned for answers. We didn't understand Josh's breathing issues, and cold weather signaled the beginning of another croup season. As for Kayla's problems . . . well, I wanted to believe we would eventually figure them out, and everything would be right as rain.

Several weeks after our trip to Birmingham, the children were playing in Josh's room when I heard Josh's ear-splitting screams. I entered his room, and what my eyes *saw* did not match up with what my ears had just *heard.* Kayla, not Josh, was covered in blood.

Josh was still screaming and crying; Kayla's entire face was drenched with blood, and it had dripped all down her arms, clothes, and legs. As I felt around on Kayla's head, trying to find the wound, I asked Josh if he was hurt. He told me that Kayla was hurting him, but I didn't understand why Kayla, who had blood all over her, was *not* crying, yet Josh, who *was* crying, appeared to be unharmed.

After sopping up the blood and attempting to calm Josh down, I found a dent in the top of Kayla's forehead. I covered it with a clean cloth diaper, applied pressure to try and stop the bleeding, and asked Josh to explain what had happened.

As the story poured from my three-and-a-half-year-old's lips, the pieces started to fall into place. Josh had been playing with his Duplo blocks on the Little Tikes workstation. Kayla decided she wanted one of the blocks and took it from him. This in turn upset Josh, who took the block back, and with his little plastic hammer, he hammered the corner of the block into Kayla's head. Guilt must have washed over him for hurting his sister, because he dramatically informed me that he told "Sissy, sorry." But in return she proceeded to "hammer" him with the plastic hammer. According to Josh, "It weally, weally hurt, Mama." As he told the story, Kayla watched Josh with a look on her face that said, "I'm still mad at you."

First things first: I talked to the kids again about sharing, asking nicely to play with each other's toys, and especially about *not* hurting one another when they didn't get their way. And for that matter, not hurting each other for any reason at all.

By this time the bleeding had slowed down on Kayla's head. I lifted the cloth and peeked at her scalp. There was a gash that needed stitches. Off we went to the doctor's office.

The kids were back to being best friends as they babbled to each other from their car seats. I watched them through my special child-view mirror and smiled, but it still bothered me that Kayla hadn't cried when she had received such a blow. I thought back through the past 19 months. Kayla was a stinker for sure, stubborn and a daredevil. We always called her a "tough cookie" because she would fall down, get back up, and keep going. When she learned how to walk, she would slam into the wall and bounce off as if nothing ever happened. And I learned the kiddos' rooms had to be supersafe, as in nothing to climb and only toys. I could never turn my back on her in any other area of the house because she could get into something or climb a bookshelf in half a second and have no fear while doing it. I even took her to the restroom with me because I was worried about the dangerous things she could accomplish in a short time.

Jeremy and I constantly tried to teach her to be careful, that there were consequences to disobeying (such as getting hurt or being punished with a time-out). But even with all of our consistency, Kayla was still Little Miss Independent, with quite a stubborn streak.

Add to all of that the fact that she rarely cried. Oh, she had cried a little when she was a baby, needing to communicate her need to be fed or changed, but she was normally content. She was a very helpful, intelligent, and, for the most part, obedient toddler, but her lack of fear or concern about getting hurt began to raise more than one question in my mind.

When we arrived at Dr. Anaya's office, he tried not to laugh as Josh explained that his boo-boos must have hurt worse because he cried. Josh's chubby little hand patted his sister. "She's okay, but she bleeded all over."

Dr. Anaya stitched Kayla up, and we chatted about my concerns. He reminded me that some toddlers are really tough, and we were doing a great job. That's one of the many things I loved about our doctor; he was always brutally honest yet encouraging at the same time. When he was genuinely worried, he'd tell me. Taking my cue from the pediatrician, I joined in the laughter as Josh told all the nurses the story and showed them his imaginary bruises.

Armed with lollipops and instructions not to do any more hammering, the children and I left the doctor's office.

Exhaustion was my close companion as the days passed. I constantly prayed for guidance. Guidance in what to watch for in my children, guidance in disciplining them, guidance for surviving the days. We were a happy family and busy with the church, but I knew my stamina was wearing thin.

Christmas Lights Are Not Candy

Right before Christmas a friend came over to watch the children so Jeremy and I could attend a Christmas party with the teens. As I began to show her where everything was, I realized I didn't have Kayla with me. I raced back to the living room, knowing that the 60 seconds we were gone could have dire consequences for my ever-inquisitive, always-a-daredevil almost-two-year-old. Josh could play contentedly for hours with simple things and never try to leap off the tallest bookshelf and pretend he could fly. Kayla, on the other hand? Yeah. Well, I watched her like a hawk.

I rounded the corner into the living room and spotted her. She was standing ever so casually in the middle of the floor, chomping furiously on something. I held my hand in front of her and firmly told Kayla to spit it out. Two green plastic pieces came out between her lips, so I pulled them from her mouth. To my horror, I realized they were the bases of little Christmas-tree lightbulbs.

Forcing Kayla's mouth open, I saw blood as she continued to chew. I stuck my fingers in her mouth in an attempt to find the glass part of the bulbs. Kayla didn't seem to care and bit down on my fingers. I knew she was cutting teeth, but I had no idea she would resort to eating glass!

I sternly scolded her for biting me and convinced her to stop chewing. She obeyed but looked at me completely unfazed, even though her mouth had little cuts all in it. There was hardly any glass left in her mouth, so it scared me to think how much she had possibly swallowed.

Once again we headed to the emergency room. I explained to the doctors what had happened, and they checked her. To everyone's amazement, she seemed to have chomped the glass down to fine dust and had no side effects or problems. They sent us home within the hour and told us to watch her—as if we hadn't heard that one before. One doctor stopped me and, with a smirk, said, "I know it's not an amusing situation now, but we're all impressed with the toughness of your daughter. Nothing seems to rattle her. It'll be a great story for the grandkids one day." He patted my shoulder and walked away chuckling and shaking his head.

As soon as we arrived home, I went to the tree. We had purchased special safety lights so the kids couldn't pull the bulbs out without pushing in a catch. *I* couldn't even get them apart without Jeremy's help, so how on earth did Kayla? The words of the doctor bounced around in my brain. *Story for the grandkids, huh? That's if I survive motherhood!* Sighing in frustration, I took all the lights off the tree.

In the month of December, Kayla's eczema worsened. It was easy to tell her to stop scratching during the day, and she listened. But at night it was a different story. By the day after Christmas, I had resorted to placing tube socks on her arms over her sleeper to see if she wouldn't scratch so hard in her sleep. But a few days later, she had dug holes in her back, through the socks and through the sleeper. I'd go in to get her out of her crib, and her sleeper would be on, with the tube socks still in place. It scared me to think how hard she scratched to do that much damage to herself.

I called Dr. Anaya and asked him what we should do. None of the creams seemed to help, and for some reason, she scratched herself until she bled—literally mutilating herself. He asked me to try a couple more things, and if the itching didn't improve over the weekend, we would have to bring her in.

The beginning of 1999 started with Kayla in the pediatrician's office undergoing a burn treatment because the wounds were so bad. That was the only way to get the skin to heal. Dr. Anaya asked one of his nurses and me to hold Kayla down while he applied the first cream. He informed me it would sting, but he couldn't do anything about the pain factor.

Dr. Anaya put on his gloves and went to work. Kayla never even flinched. I shared a glance with the doctor, and as soon as he was done, he asked the nurse to sit with Kayla while he and I talked.

I followed him out the door, and in the hallway he explained to me that we weren't going to wait until Kayla passed the age of two to see a neurologist. He wanted to set up an appointment as quickly as he could, because all the pieces were finally adding up—Kayla's inability to sweat, her overheating, her lack of fear, her "toughness," the block-and-hammer incident, the lightbulb episode, and now the unresponsive reaction to the burn treatment. I knew immediately by the look on his face that this was serious. We needed to get some answers.

You know, on some of those darkest days postpartum, I felt really bad for questioning God. And when we had to keep waiting for more tests and more doctors, and still no diagnosis, I would again question *why*. Had I done something wrong? Had I done everything I possibly could for my children? Had I missed something?

I was mentally criticizing myself in that hallway when Dr. Anaya laid his hand on my shoulder.

"Mrs. Woodhouse," he said, "we're close. We'll find the answers. Stop beating yourself up. You've done a great job."

How did he know what I'd been thinking?

But then I felt the Lord's presence, His comfort, and that still, small voice telling me to wait on Him. I didn't need the answers right then, although I wanted them. Sometimes we have to wait on Him for days; other times it's a year or two—or more. But if we truly seek Him, He gives us the strength, peace, and *joy* to wait.

An Angel Named Sarah

Sarah Moody became one of my closest friends. God had indeed brought us an angel when He brought her into our lives. She would call to check up on us, make sure the KoolVest was working properly, and call doctors at NASA to see if anyone could help diagnose our little Kayla.

Sarah laughed with me, cried with me, prayed with me. Her own personal story was amazing, but how she started, ran, and raised money for the HED Foundation could inspire anyone to reach out to another hurting human being.

I knew each and every day that I was so blessed to have her in my life.

And I told her that if I ever had a chance, I wanted to give back so they could help more and more children like our own sweet Kayla.

As we all waited for the neurological appointment, Sarah was there every step of the way. With her cheery disposition she reminded me that there were other children who needed help, other parents going through similar difficult circumstances. She asked me if I would be willing to help encourage others through phone calls and e-mail. And a better gift she couldn't have given me.

All these years I'd wondered what gifts I had to use. Music had been my forte for many years—it's what I'd studied all my life—but through Sarah I understood that there was more I could offer.

You see, Sarah understood giving rather than receiving. She called me and gave me phone numbers of other families. Many of these people had no hope. The threat of their child's illness, medical bills, and prognosis dragged them down. But with each phone call I made to offer empathy and encouragement—through tears and God's grace—they were lifted up. As I gave of myself to support other parents, I, in turn, was refreshed.

Fearfully and Wonderfully Made

April breezed in faster than we expected, and with it our appointment at the pediatric neurologist's office. As we made the drive to the Arkansas Children's Hospital in Little Rock, I prayed for the outcome and my willingness to consider it pure joy. James 1:2–4 still jumped out at me and screamed, "This is what you need to learn!" How many reminders had I needed up to this point?

So, like the never-prone-to-worry Super-Christian that I am—hold your laughter—I memorized those verses in the car. That took minimal effort. Yes! I had arrived. What a great testimony I had! Since the drive was a long one, I practiced on my husband and children.

"Whew!" I said to myself as I wiped the sweat off my forehead. "Next lesson, please!" (You really should be laughing with me at this point.)

Triumphant that I had completed my assignment as we entered the hospital parking lot, I just knew I was ready to face the day. We hauled the children and Kayla's cooling gear inside and settled in to wait for our appointment. After about an hour, we were ushered into a room to see Dr. Terence Edgar. When we met, I instantly liked this doctor and his delightful South African accent.

Dr. Edgar asked me to start at the very beginning and give him every detail I could remember. It took more than an hour to discuss all of Kayla's issues, doctors' appointments, and tests.

By the time I finished, the kind doctor just looked at me and smiled.

"I know exactly what is wrong with Kayla, and I will explain it to you right now."

I was shocked and just a little skeptical at his words. I mean, really, after all this time, this new doctor figured it out? Just like that? And he was *smiling* about it?

He must have sensed my doubt because he began with, "Mr. and Mrs. Woodhouse, I know that you have traveled a long road. And the search for answers has not been easy. But you needed to travel each of these steps for us to get to this point. Each place, each test, each incident have all been important to reaching the conclusions drawn today. I have a diagnosis for your daughter, and I believe you will be relieved. But *do* understand this information will be tough to grasp. You will have a lot of questions, and there won't be a lot of help for you because of the rarity of this condition."

Jeremy and I glanced at each other, and then at the children. Then Jeremy smiled at me and nodded. He looked relieved. I felt . . . well . . . scared.

The doctor continued, "I believe Kayla has a rare nerve disorder called hereditary sensory autonomic neuropathy. There are fibers missing in the postganglionic sympathetic nerve, so matters of intensity are not correctly signaled to the brain. In other words, when Kayla is getting too hot, the nerve does not signal the brain the intensity, thus she doesn't sweat. When Kayla gets hurt, the nerve doesn't signal the brain the intensity, and so she doesn't cry. When Kayla feels the itch of her eczema, she scratches but cannot tell the intensity of how hard she is scratching."

It all sounded so simple, and yet it went completely over my head. I blurted, "Is there anything we can do?"

Dr. Edgar patted my knee. "No."

"Is there a cure? Can't you fix it?"

"No."

"Is there a chance she'll grow out of this? Ever?"

Dr. Edgar rolled his stool very close. "Mom, are you looking at me?"

I looked at Jeremy instead.

The fact that the doctor was calling me Mom made me think about my children, and they were watching me. What incredible tactical skills this man had. He had me cornered, and he knew it. "Mom, you need to listen."

Reluctantly I turned my head and with tear-filled eyes looked at the doctor. "Yes, sir."

"You will probably never meet another person with this disorder. You will probably never meet a doctor who's even seen it. Kayla will live with this, and she will be fine. If I had to choose a nerve disorder to have, it would be this one."

He squeezed my hand and rolled away to grab a box of tissues for me. "You have done a great job keeping her alive. Just do your best, and I will give you all the information I can to help."

I blew my nose and wiped my face. Kayla sat in Jeremy's lap playing with a stuffed parrot Dr. Edgar had given her. Breathing deeply, I turned back to the doctor.

"Okay. So what do we need to do?"

He laughed. "Atta girl! I knew you could do it. Well, first I have a question. How did she not suffer heat stroke as a tiny baby?" He glanced at his notes. "You mentioned you lived even farther south than here. I'm amazed she's alive."

I explained my postpartum struggles to the doctor, and the overwhelming sense of joy filled my insides once again.

God had spared Kayla's life.

The Agony to Feel No Pain

Kayla sat in my lap while our specialist tested his theory. He poked, he prodded, he pinched. At one point, he pinched the inside of Kayla's thigh and twisted, and I thought Jeremy would come out of his chair and slug the poor man, protective father that he is. But thankfully, he didn't. Dr. Edgar must have noticed our discomfort with his methods because he began to explain what he was testing. Kayla could feel the slightest touch, but the harder you patted, pinched, or pulled didn't make any difference to her. This made sense. We knew she could feel the itch of the eczema, but she didn't appear to notice how hard she scratched herself.

After he was satisfied with his findings, Dr. Edgar informed us that Kayla would need to be evaluated by a nerve-conduction study to confirm the diagnosis. She would be sedated for the test, because steel pins would be inserted into the skin, through the muscle, to the nerves. That way doctors could monitor the conduction of information to the brain. The test would show to what extent Kayla *did* feel.

The cases Dr. Edgar had read about said the intensity level would need to be 100 times the intensity a "normal" person would feel for it to register with a hereditary sensory autonomic neuropathy (HSAN) patient like Kayla. Dr. Edgar wasn't convinced this was the case, but he wanted to be sure.

Before we left, he gave us instructions about toys, heaters, stoves, ovens, and ice. The illustration he gave that has stuck with me ever since was about a stovetop. If you or I were to touch a hot burner on a stove, we would pull away immediately. In Kayla's case, she could touch the burner and leave her hand there because it would not register pain until severe damage was done.

Wow. No wonder Kayla was a daredevil and appeared to have no fear. The dots were connecting, and pieces of our crazy puzzle were falling into place.

Hours later, we were in the car on the way home. Jeremy was thrilled with the news and told me how great it felt to finally have a diagnosis and have that burden off his shoulders.

But me? I sat and sulked in my seat.

Jeremy pulled off the interstate to fill the car up with gas, but as he put the car in park, he grabbed my hand and made me look at him. "What's bugging you, honey?"

My lips trembled, and tears streamed down my cheeks. "My baby," I sputtered, "she has to deal with this the rest of her life . . ." I dramatically relayed information he already knew. "And . . . and I can't fix it!"

Jeremy, my ever-present, steady, levelheaded, logical husband, *laughed*. At me.

But with love and mild sarcasm shining in his eyes, he asked me, "Um, honey? What were those verses you memorized this morning?"

Ouch. Talk about getting my attention.

To intensify my conviction, Kayla babbled from the backseat, "It's okay, Mama. It's okay."

Jeremy got out and pumped the gas, while I sat pondering their words. They were both right. Everything came gushing into my brain like a giant tidal wave. Yes, God was in control. Yes, this was a trial. Yes, life had been hard. And yes, I wanted some miracle cure. But joy was still there for the taking. And I had to persevere. I just hadn't learned my lesson . . . yet.

Intensity Multiplied by 30

I called Sarah Moody the next day, and she helped me work through the load of information that had been dumped in my lap. As we researched together, my heart lightened because of Sarah's ability to encourage and make others laugh.

Life moved forward. The nerve-conduction study was several weeks away, but when the time came, I was ready. My family traveled once again to the children's hospital in Little Rock, where doctors sedated Kayla and began the test. Information flashed across the screens, and Dr. Edgar tried to explain to me what we were seeing. All of a sudden, Kayla sat up.

Dr. Edgar jumped into action. "Take note, Mom, Kayla does not sedate."

"What does *that* mean?" I asked as I rushed to her side.

Kayla looked frustrated and dazed, and was attempting to pull the pins out of her body. But we calmed her down, and Dr. Edgar and the nurses tried it again.

"It means," the doctor continued, "that you need to remember she doesn't react well to sedation. She should be 'out'—still asleep." He smiled as if to ease the news. "I should have guessed that Kayla would do something unexpected."

Okay, then. I found myself giggling; of course Kayla wouldn't fit into a medical box. She'd never done anything the way we anticipated. I had no idea what any of it really meant, but I made a mental note anyway.

"Good news." Dr. Edgar's comment broke through my reverie.

"I believe that Kayla will register pain, heat, or cold if it's 20 to 30 times the intensity, rather than 100 times. We can be very thankful for that." He pulled me closer to the monitors and pointed. "Look, she has some of the fibers here and here."

I tried to follow his finger to see and possibly understand what he was talking about. Complicated as it was, the screens began to make sense. Partly because hearing "good news" is every parent's dream—and the other part I attributed to my brain registering that 20 to 30 was incredibly better than 100.

The test concluded, and a little later I sat in the doctor's office listening to his explanation. We would need to keep Kayla in an environment under 68 degrees and be diligent in watching and observing for signs of physical stress. If she took a hard fall, we would need to check for broken bones. Kayla would need to wear a MedicAlert bracelet in case of an accident, because she wouldn't be able to accurately assess what she was feeling.

Overall, Dr. Edgar appeared pleased with the results, and I felt relief with that knowledge. Kayla snuggled close in my lap, holding on to my hand, and smiled.

The doctor came around his desk and sat on the chair next to me. "God has special plans for this little one," he said. "He knows what He's doing. Always keep that in mind."

Psalm 139

Our amazing neurologist will probably never know how much his words helped me. Once again I needed to see the bigger picture and set my sights on things above. Colossians 3:2 came barreling into my brain: "Set your mind on the things above, not on the things that are on earth" (NASB). I didn't understand God's infinite plan. I didn't know what would happen the next minute, much less the next day. And yet just like the time when

I didn't understand my postpartum depression, I didn't have to understand what God's plan was for my life or Kayla's life or Josh's life or Jeremy's life. I just needed to keep my sights set on things above. God was in control, and I'd never be able to fathom the incredible path that lay ahead.

As the days flew by, we continued with our indoor life. So many wonderful people helped us along the way with gift cards, toys for the kids, and lots of indoor activities. I realized we'd been living this way for more than a year. It was already habit, so why had I been so worried when I heard the diagnosis and about Kayla living with this for the rest of her life?

Josh and Kayla were thriving and had no trouble with the restrictions because it was our "normal." *My* issue was that my children were vastly opposite. I worried about Kayla missing out on so much of life because she would be cloistered in a 68-degree prison, and I worried about Josh missing out because so much of our family's time, money, and energy were spent dealing with Kayla's disorder. All parents want the best for their children, and I felt that what I was offering came up short.

But one day during my devotions, I opened my Bible to Psalm 139. As I made my way through the chapter, my heart cried out to the Lord.

> O LORD, you have searched me
> and you know me. (verse 1)

Okay, thank You for the reminder, Lord. You know me better than I know myself.

> You know when I sit and when I rise;
> you perceive my thoughts from afar. (verse 2)

You understand better than anyone what happens in my life day after day. And You know my heart and my worries; You know my children, their needs, and their desires.

> You discern my going out and my lying down;
>> you are familiar with all my ways. (verse 3)

Even when I fail, or feel like I'm failing as a mom, You are there to lift me up.

> Before a word is on my tongue
>> you know it completely, O LORD. (verse 4)

Ouch, I guess no more whining or complaining, huh?

> You hem me in—behind and before;
>> you have laid your hand upon me. (verse 5)

You have tried to get my attention, constantly telling me You are there, always there to comfort me, and yet I struggle with doubts.

> Such knowledge is too wonderful for me,
>> too lofty for me to attain. (verse 6)

I know I don't deserve it, but wow, Lord, You are so cool.

> Where can I go from your Spirit?
>> Where can I flee from your presence? (verse 7)

No matter how far I run, You are there. I've been running from difficult circumstances, not wanting to face them with joy.

> If I go up to the heavens, you are there;
>> if I make my bed in the depths, you are there.
>>> (verse 8)

You love me when I'm praising You, and You love me when I'm having a pity party.

> If I rise on the wings of the dawn,
>> if I settle on the far side of the sea,
> even there your hand will guide me,
>> your right hand will hold me fast. (verses 9–10)

Keep reminding me, Lord—I know I'm hardheaded.

> If I say, "Surely the darkness will hide me
>> and the light become night around me,"
> even the darkness will not be dark to you;
>> the night will shine like the day,
>> for darkness is as light to you. (verses 11–12)

And even my darkest times can be filled with joy. Why can't I learn this lesson?

> For you created my inmost being;
>> you knit me together in my mother's womb.
>>> (verse 13)

You knew what You were doing when You made Josh and Kayla. You knew what they would endure, and You created them for a purpose. Banish my fear, Lord. Take it away. You are in control. The doctors don't have to have all the answers because I know that You do, and I will trust in that.

I praise you because I am fearfully and wonderfully made;
> your works are wonderful,
> I know that full well.
My frame was not hidden from you
> when I was made in the secret place.
When I was woven together in the depths of the earth,
> your eyes saw my unformed body.
All the days ordained for me
> were written in your book
> before one of them came to be. (verses 14–16)

You gave me Josh and Kayla. You've given me what I need to be their mom. Thank You for reminding me that I am Your creation, and Your works are wonderful.

How precious to me are your thoughts, O God!
> How vast is the sum of them!
Were I to count them,
> they would outnumber the grains of sand.
When I awake,
> I am still with you. (verses 17–18)

Isn't God cool? His Scripture is exactly what we need for every moment, every trial, and every tribulation. And even though we may have read something or heard something over and over in our lives, we still need those reminders.

The end of Psalm 139 is something I go over every day now:

> Search me, O God, and know my heart;
> > test me and know my anxious thoughts.
> See if there is any offensive way in me,
> > and lead me in the way everlasting. (verses 23–24)

The way everlasting. That's our goal, isn't it? Each and every day should be focused on worshipping God in everything, giving Him the glory for everything, and focusing on things of eternal value, not those things that will fade away.

CHAPTER FOUR

Trial by Fire

The trials kept coming. A few months after Kayla was diagnosed, I woke abruptly in the middle of the night. Josh couldn't breathe. I could hear his gasps all the way down the hall.

Jeremy and I both ran to his room. I pulled on my bathrobe as I ran, and Jeremy grabbed the car keys. We were supposed to be leaving early in the morning to help one of the church's teens, and we had a babysitter spending the night so we wouldn't have to wake up the kiddos when we left. My words spilled out in a jumble. I told her we were headed to the emergency room and asked her to keep an eye on Kayla, and then we raced out the door with Josh.

When we arrived at the hospital, a nurse gave Josh a breathing treatment at the doctor's order, and then she placed us in a room to wait. No one took his breathing difficulties seriously because according to the books, children Josh's age should be able to breathe through croup. It was a small town, the ER was busy, and *no one* would listen.

A doctor finally came to see us as the sun rose. He looked at Josh's chart and told us we should go home. Josh would be fine, he said.

Mama bear came out. I should have prayed first, because I scared the living daylights out of the poor man. I informed him that Josh had had several episodes of croup that landed him in PICU; they didn't know the cause, but his airway would close up, and he couldn't breathe. I asked him to call our pediatrician, Dr. Anaya.

"Ma'am, we can handle this situation, there's no need—"

Interrupting, I pointed to Josh, who was laboring for breath in bed. "Quite frankly, I don't think you can, and for your information, I didn't come to the ER in the middle of the night, in my pajamas, for *fun!*"

Yes, I lost it. Imagine that—a mom losing it, in her pajamas, finally getting someone's attention. Novel concept. (I don't recommend it.)

Reluctantly the doctor admitted Josh to the hospital.

Later that morning no one had come to check on my little guy, and I was getting concerned. His breathing was shallow and his coloring a sickly gray. I buzzed the nurse, who came quickly.

Completely exhausted, I sobbed all over the poor woman while explaining Josh's problems. She looked shocked that we had been there for hours, and no one had helped us. As she leaned over Josh to take his vitals, his raspy breathing turned into that horrid croupy cough, and he went into distress. And then my sweet baby threw up all over the one person who was trying to help.

I've never been more impressed by a person in the medical profession. She took it all in stride, wiped herself off while she rang for more help and gave Josh another breathing treatment. She didn't leave the room until he could breathe easily on his own.

Not more than 20 minutes later, Dr. Anaya came racing into the room. And after a quick discussion with him, within another 20 minutes an ear, nose, and throat (ENT) specialist arrived.

Dr. Anaya spoke quietly to me as I narrowed my gaze at this new doctor. "Mrs. Woodhouse," he said, "I'm so sorry that others of our profession have acted so unprofessionally, and with such ill regard for your son." He took my hand and continued, "But I assure you, we are here to help Josh and figure out the nature of his difficulties." I nodded, and the ENT doc took a look at Josh. Time passed slowly, until finally the doctor stated, "Oh, my."

Dr. Anaya and I quickly came to the specialist's side. Josh lay on the bed lethargically.

"Mrs. Woodhouse," said Dr. ENT, "Josh's trachea is half the size it should be. That's why he can't breathe when he gets sick. Essentially, it swells up and swells shut."

I sat down really hard on the edge of the bed. The doctor continued to explain, but I didn't listen. Something else? Goodness, haven't I gone through enough, Lord? I have a child with a really rare nerve disorder, and now I'll always worry that every time my son gets sick, he might stop breathing!

Somehow, my whining to God didn't help.

The ENT doctor cleared his throat. "Mrs. Woodhouse? Did you hear me? Josh will need surgery, and soon. I think we can make more room by stretching it and taking out his tonsils and adenoids. He'll need tubes in his ears as well."

I squeaked, "Surgery? How soon?"

"Let me try to fit it in next week. I'll call my office."

I thanked him, Dr. Anaya squeezed my shoulder, and the two of them left the room.

Once Josh was discharged, we went home with breathing treatments and instructions for the next week. As the days passed, I went through our normal routine and arranged for our time at the hospital, seemingly with everything under control.

The day came for Josh's surgery. They took him to surgery, and Jeremy sat with me in the waiting room. And wouldn't you know? James 1:2–4 kept popping into my head, but I pushed those verses back. I knew them in my head; I didn't need to repeat them over and over. Or so I thought.

When the surgeon came out and informed us the surgery was a success and Josh was doing incredibly well, I smiled, and then I cried. Why? Because all of a sudden, I knew the reason God kept bringing those words to mind.

Yes, I had obediently learned the verses, but I hadn't applied them. I was willing to have joy when everything was all right, but not when I was in the midst of the trial. And you know what? God *really* wanted me to learn that lesson.

Oh, boy.

Power Problem

A few months later, Jeremy began working at a wonderful little church in south Louisiana. We wanted to be closer to family so I could have help with the kids. Located close to an army post, the church had a large percentage of military members. We had been so blessed by the friends and wonderful teens we'd worked with over the years, and this church was no different.

The Lord blessed us in an amazing way through the people in our new church. Dr. Patricia Carter and her husband, Dr. Scott Carter, were some of the first to reach out to us. Trish and I became close instantly, and her kids, who were almost the same ages as Josh and Kayla, befriended my pair. The Sunday-school teachers were quick to learn all the details about Kayla's needs. They prepared the Sunday-school room so she could attend class with the other kids. One couple from church offered their pool for Kayla to swim in during the hot months so she could do something outside. And Deanna Chang was so like me in personality, it made me wonder if she was my twin, separated at birth.

As people came and went in the military community, we made some of the best friends of our lives. The newspaper and news stations did features on Kayla's story, and I grew comfortable talking publicly about her disorder. With lots of wonderful people surrounding us with love and care, as well as helping hands, I felt safe. I had no idea I was about to get the lesson of my life.

One Friday night I was getting ready to leave for Bible study. Josh had just turned five, and Kayla was now three years old, so it was always fun trying to get *out* the door. Amanda, a great friend who had been coming to an Officer's Christian Fellowship (OCF) Bible study we hosted in our home, called about the ladies' Bible study and asked if she could come. I told her all about our great fellowship and the time of spiritual refreshment as I packed up the car with sippy cups, toys, diaper bag, and of course, children. As soon as I hung up the phone, the power went out.

"Oh, great! This can't be good; I'm already running behind," I said to myself. I was the pastor's wife and the Bible-study teacher—I couldn't be late. "What do I do now?"

My two precious babies just looked at me as if they were thinking, *It's dark, Mommy is talking to herself, and she's supposed to have all the answers.*

Problem number one: how do you open the garage door when there is no power?

Hmm . . . I don't know. So I pressed the button, somehow thinking there might just be enough juice left to open it. I was wrong.

I called my husband, but he was still up at the church and couldn't come home before I needed to leave. He did the logical thing. He gave me instructions—in man language.

"Sure, honey, I understand," I replied. Yeah, uh-huh. Not really.

Problem number two: how do you see where you're going in a pitch-black garage with no flashlight?

Well, let's see . . . I tripped over the dog, who had now been traumatized and proceeded to relieve himself on the floor; I then continued on and stepped (wearing socks) in the puddle, only to find I would have to climb on top of the car to pull the cord thingy that released the whatchamacallit so the garage door could open.

Problem number three: I had memorized James 1:2–4, and God wouldn't leave me alone about it. What did those verses *really* mean? And why were they coming to mind when I was in the middle of a crisis? (Gosh, who actually thought about application? Don't answer that.)

I stopped in my tracks (literally) and began to quote the Scripture. "Consider it pure joy, pure joy, pure *joy* . . . whenever you face *trials* of many kinds!" I laughed. "Okay, God, I get it. This is great." Even if joy includes stepping in dog pee? Giggle. The answer is yes!

I smiled and told my kids we were going to praise God and consider it joy whenever we had problems. So we started singing "Jesus Loves Me" while I attempted to climb on top of the Camry in the dark. My eyes had adjusted somewhat to the lack of light, but not enough to make a difference in figuring out the mechanics of an electric garage-door opener while I balanced precariously on top of my car. Midway through the chorus, my adorable little boy, in his cute little voice, asked, "Mommy? You okay?"

I laughed. Really hard. What a way to learn a lesson about joy through trials. There I was, on top of the car, in a garage with no windows, in my dog-puddle-drenched socks, singing with my children. We continued to sing as I *un*gracefully slid off the roof of the car and landed in a dismount position any gymnast would have been proud of (at least in wet socks). My children could see me because the cab light illuminated the inside of the car. They clapped as I bowed humbly before them. Unbuckling the car seats, I picked up my kiddos, and with one on each hip, I decided it was time to change tactics.

After giving up on the garage door, I changed my socks, scrubbed my feet and hands, and called Amanda.

Laughing, I asked her, "You still want to come to Bible study? The teacher needs a ride!"

What a great sport. Amanda and I were good friends, so I knew she was incredible before this. But my respect and admiration for her would grow as the next 24 hours progressed.

She graciously picked us up, and off we went to Bible study. And what a time we had. I shared with the ladies about my little adventure and how the Lord had used it to teach me an incredible lesson. That poor group of women! We went through two boxes of tissues because we laughed so hard, we cried.

I went on with my serious question. What good was memorizing Scripture if I couldn't apply it to my life? How long had I kept those verses locked inside? I challenged the ladies to work on the verses with me, to hide them in their hearts and really learn them. And I warned them to watch out for the adventures along the way.

Perseverance?

Amanda brought the kids and me home, and I realized there was still no power. Oh, bother, now we *really* have a problem. We lived in south Louisiana. My daughter doesn't sweat. No power meant *no* air-conditioning. I had several moments of "Okay, so now what?" as we sat in the cool car.

Jeremy came out to the vehicle, we ran down the list of needs and objectives, and he helped make some quick decisions. Amanda volunteered to go with us to a hotel. Jeremy would stay home, wait for the power to come back on, and let us know when the house was cooled down.

Armed with a plan, I went inside, packed a bag, and kissed my hubby goodnight. We've never liked being apart, so I inwardly wished it could all be fixed instantaneously, but I knew I needed to get Kayla to a cooler place.

Arriving at the hotel, I faced yet another trial. The air-conditioning wasn't working in our room. I tried to laugh at the situation as the manager called maintenance. But after finding out it would take awhile to fix, and then the room had to cool down, I had to make another decision. Sit in the air-conditioned car while we waited or go swimming.

We chose swimming.

As the night melted into the wee hours of the morning, I began to tire. I wanted direction from God. We all wish at some point or other that a magical instructional guide will zoom down from heaven. I've even begged and pleaded for heavenly sticky notes. "Please, Lord! Just a little one. Let me know if I'm headed even remotely in the right direction!" I always envisioned one of those notes flying through the window, smacking into my forehead, and sticking there. I looked to the sky for my handy little sticky note, and when it didn't come, I started going through the verses again. Joy and perseverance and faith were hard when I was tired . . . and grumpy.

The children were laughing and playing in the water when my son looked up at me and asked, "Mommy, should we sing some more? Do you need more joy?"

Out of the mouths of babes. My son figured out the joy in trials and the value of perseverance before *I* did. Wow. Imagine if I had listened years ago.

More? I didn't think I wanted to learn any more.

A True Test of Faith

Saturday would be the true testing of my faith. I was tired. I was cranky. And I had learned two very good lessons. That *really* should be enough for any young mother to handle in a few short hours.

I was wrong.

My husband had called early that morning to tell me the power had indeed come back on, but we should probably wait until lunchtime to make sure the house would be cool enough. This was perfectly fine with me, since we hadn't gone to bed until after 2:00 AM, and we were all pretty tired.

After our "slumber party" and a leisurely morning at the hotel, Amanda brought us home. Again.

I invited her over for dinner that night to thank her for all she'd done to help. She headed home to get some things done but promised to come back in a couple of hours. I had already missed a good portion of my day, so I set to work on my constant list of things to do.

Laundry was first and foremost on the list. I normally did a load or two every day, but Saturday was always my big laundry day when I did all the sheets, bath mats, towels, and clothes. The kids' laundry hampers were the first ones to be hauled to the laundry room, and I dumped their contents on the floor. My husband gave me a quick hug and kiss and headed out to visit an elderly lady in our church. Having just transferred the first load to the dryer, I sorted and threw clothes into the washing machine for the second load. I pulled some chicken out of the freezer and put it in the microwave to defrost.

I had one more hamper to empty—the one in our bedroom, which was on the other end of our large ranch-style home. By the time I retrieved the hamper and made it back to the kitchen area, the smell of smoke hung in the air.

"That's odd," I murmured.

I quickly yanked the chicken out of the microwave, thinking the large, old model must have reached its end. But the chicken was fine, and there was no smoke. It was then I noticed the dog trying to paw his way under the laundry-room door. Large wisps of smoke floated up to my face. The chicken forgotten, I flung it in the sink and opened the door. Smoke was everywhere. Thick, nasty, cough-inducing smoke. The dog took off running and barking. I choked and sputtered.

The only logical conclusion I could come to was that the culprit was the dryer. I couldn't reach the outlet to unplug the appliance, so without thinking, I opened the dryer door. (Yes, I know, smart move.)

Flames engulfed the clothes in the drum, and I quickly slammed the door shut. Closing the door between the laundry room and the kitchen area, and then the door between the kitchen and the living room, I called my little ones and ran to the master bedroom. There I found some hand towels, wet them down, and instructed Josh and Kayla to hold them over their noses and mouths.

The smoke wasn't as bad at the other end of the house, but I knew it would quickly be coming toward us.

Problem number one: Your dryer is on fire. Enough said.

Problem number two: You couldn't care less about the dryer or the house burning to the ground. You're just trying to figure out how to get you and your children out of the house when the car is on the other side of the fiery dryer, it's 115 degrees outside, and you've called all your neighbors and none of them are home.

Problem number three: your husband's cell phone isn't in range, and you can't reach him.

Problem number four: you've had enough trials for one 24-hour period, and you're now wondering how to consider *this* pure joy.

Well, it's actually a funny story.

I smiled at Josh, and he started singing with his baby sister. As they sat there with towels over their faces, I called another lady from the church—Heidi—who lived near the lady Jeremy was visiting. She asked me a question in the sweetest voice: "Kim, have you called 911?"

"911?" I laughed at her, like what a ridiculous suggestion. "I don't care about the house. I just need to get *out* of the house!"

Heidi giggled and calmly responded, "Well, you know they can help with *that* too."

Duh. Why didn't I think of that?

She told me she would find Jeremy, and I said I would call 911. Bless her heart.

Now, I need to tell you we lived in a small town. *Small* being the operative word.

I dialed.

"Nine-one-one emergency response," a kind voice greeted me.

I spoke quickly, "My dryer is on fire, the house is filled with smoke, and I need an air-conditioned vehicle so my two children and I can get out of the house."

"What is your location?"

I gave her my address and where we were located in the house.

"Ma'am, you need to get out of the house."

"Yes, ma'am, that's what I'm trying to do."

"Ma'am, you need to get out of the house."

Hadn't she said that already?

"Yes, ma'am, I understand, but I *can't* get out of the house. That's why I need an air-conditioned vehicle," I calmly replied.

"Why can't you get out of the house?" Worry filled her voice. "Are you stuck?"

"No, ma'am. We're fine. We have wet towels over our faces, but it's 115 degrees outside, and my daughter doesn't sweat. She'll die if I take her outside."

I actually heard a little "bling," as if the lightbulb had come on and she knew exactly who we were. Kayla had been on the news and in the paper a lot, so I was thankful the dispatcher had connected the dots.

She asked me to stay on the line while she dispatched an air-conditioned car and the fire department.

Within a couple of minutes, two squad cars drove through the grass in my front yard, right up to the front door.

I opened the door, armed with diaper bags, Kayla's cooling gear, and two small children. The young officer from the first car stood there in a stance very much like a football player about to catch the winning touch-down pass.

"Throw me the child!" he instructed me.

I couldn't help it. I laughed.

I walked my children to the car, and he put Kayla in the front seat so the vents would be blowing on her. While his intentions were good, I in-formed him that putting my daughter up front probably wasn't the smartest of choices. As soon as the words left my mouth, the sirens in his cruiser were blaring, and lights were flashing. Yep, Little Smarty had dis-covered the differences between Mommy's car and a police car with lots of gadgets. Josh was giggling in the backseat, jumping up and down, screaming, "More!!! More!!!" It was then I decided to move my younger child before she tried to drive away. (And she probably could have.)

The police scurried around, taking good care of us, and soon, up pulled the fire truck. Pretty soon another one appeared. Did I mention this is a small town? I was amazed.

They managed to get the garage door open, and smoke billowed out. Their next dilemma was removing the car. One officer asked me to step off to the side and said, "Ma'am, we really don't want the house to blow up, so we need your keys." I told them exactly where they were—on the kitchen counter.

Five minutes and three officers later, there was more smoke, and still no success with the car keys. I am meticulous about these things, so their lack of ability in obtaining the keys made me impatient. Did they even listen when I explained the keys' whereabouts?

Exasperated and in a huff, I told them I would go get them myself. This didn't go over well, and I was met with a wall of tall uniformed firemen. I was given a stern lecture on the dangers of smoke inhalation and told that absolutely under no circumstances was I to enter the house.

So when they turned their attention from discussing *why* I couldn't go back in to *how* they were going to move the car, I snuck in with my wet towel over my face and came out with the keys.

Thankful as they were to be able to move the car, I got the "look" from the head fireman dude and realized how dumb I had just been. And I had managed to lose it in front of them. I mean, they were, after all, there to help me—and *I* lost my patience.

Suddenly the end of James 1:2–4 came springing to my mind: " . . . perseverance must finish its work so that you may be mature and complete, not lacking anything." Wow. Mature and complete. I mumbled, "Mature and complete, mature and complete . . ."

Hanging my head in shame, I prayed. *Lord, why You ever put up with me, I'll never know. But thank You for loving me enough to teach me these hard lessons.*

Amanda drove up in the middle of the chaos. Laughing, she stepped out of her car and asked, "Life is always an adventure with you, isn't it?"

I laughed with her and cried as I relayed the events of the afternoon, feeling my remorse all the way down to my toes.

"I really want to be mature and complete!" I sobbed.

After a good cry and an even better laughing-till-you-cry fest, I sat in the grass watching the firemen pull the charred remains of my dryer from the house. I told Amanda how thankful I was that the Lord had brought me through the past 24 hours.

God didn't direct the bad things to happen. He doesn't sit up there on a great big throne and say, "Let's see what I can put Kim through today!"

No.

We live in a sin-filled world, and yes, bad things are going to happen.

But He did use those circumstances for my good. He used my trials to teach me that His joy is mine for the taking. It's there. I know. Because I felt it and grabbed on to it.

Little did I know, 10 years later I'd still be working on always finding the joy. But it has become my steadfast companion—and James 1:2–4, my life verses.

CHAPTER FIVE

Alaska? Are You Serious?

After the fire we cleaned up the damage and moved on with life. Jeremy was superbusy with the church. He did everything from funerals to weddings, preaching to directing preschoolers. And my time was filled with the kiddos, women's Bible study, and all the music for the church. We'd also chosen to homeschool, so life was very full.

Our new pediatrician set Kayla up with several specialists to see what could be done to help heal her eczema. A few times she had scratched so badly, she reopened wounds and eventually had a staph infection. The eczema flared so intensely that every day it was a challenge to keep the areas clean, prevent her from scratching, and cream her with the prescription ointments.

"You should move to a place like Alaska," all the doctors quipped. I don't remember how many different doctors told us that within a six-month span, but it wasn't funny after the first dozen times. The dermatologist came to that conclusion after telling us we needed to lower the temperature Kayla lived in to 65 degrees. The warmer she was, the more inflamed her eczema became, and the more she scratched. The neurologist agreed, saying that she would function better in a lower temperature.

But what finally caught my attention was the allergy specialist performing tests on Kayla. She had 144 tests total. And she was allergic to almost everything. Severely.

The doctor was reading the results of a panel of pricks on Kayla's back and labeled the first set a "4," which was the highest number he could assign. But by the time he finished the entire panel and looked back, that patch had doubled in size. He glanced up at me and smiled, and I knew we were on our way to another adventure.

Dust mites.

I'd heard of them, knew what they were, but I assure you I did *not* want to become privy to the details of their filthy microscopic lives.

My skin crawls just thinking about it.

Dust mites love warmth and high humidity. And we had lots of both. We not only needed to control the temperature in Kayla's environment, but there could be no more stuffed animals, no upholstered furniture, no carpet, no clothing that couldn't be washed in hot water. Mattresses and pillows had to be encased in special coverings, and she could only sleep on sheets with a high thread count. Dehumidifiers would have to be bought and run constantly, and maintaining a low humidity level would be vital to controlling this icky little allergen called dust mites.

Thank goodness I am a clean freak. I was already in the habit of washing all the sheets, shower curtains, and bath mats once a week. (Remember the vast amounts of laundry during the dryer fire incident?) I vacuumed every day just because the kids were little and I wanted to keep their play areas clean. Little did I know that all of this had helped Kayla, but it would need to continue at an even more rigorous pace.

We also had to deal with the new information and results from all the other tests. Kayla had some serious, and I mean *serious,* allergies. The doctor and I hashed things out for more than an hour, and the best plan of action we could come up with was to change as much environmentally as we could. Since she was allergic to so many foods and had been eating them all her life, we were hesitant to completely remove them from her diet. If we drastically changed her diet, but then she ate a trace of an allergen, she could have an adverse reaction. The doctor was compassionate, understanding that Kayla's short life was already vastly different from other children her age, but he advised us that we had to make more changes nonetheless.

This doctor again jokingly stated that we should move to Alaska. Yeah, right. Alaska? Where everyone lives in an igloo, there's snow year-round, and the sun doesn't shine for six months? Please. My ignorance tainted my thoughts.

The kids and I traveled home to deliver the news to Jeremy. As I walked through the house, I was overwhelmed with the thought of everything that needed to be cleaned, replaced, or tossed, but I told myself I could be joyful in the process. Facing the additional costs wouldn't be easy, but if it improved Kayla's health, it would be worth it.

Two days later, a pastor friend called for Jeremy while I was washing the dishes. Slinging the dish towel over my shoulder, I took the phone outside to my husband, who was working on an old boat. I stood by Jeremy, admired his handiwork, and basked in the sun. As soon as he hung up, Jeremy looked at me and laughed. "You won't believe what that phone call was about."

"What?"

"Well, there's a mission in Alaska that our friend just put my name in for. Isn't that a riot? All these doctors joke about us moving to Alaska, and then we get a phone call about it."

I laughed along with him but inwardly cringed. Surely he wasn't seriously thinking about this. "So what did you say?"

"I told him that was fine, and we'll see where the Lord leads."

Being the unfaltering Christian who never complains, worries, or balks at what life brings, I responded with duplicitous cheeriness, "That's great, honey. You never know what God is going to do."

He handed me the phone and kissed me on the cheek, and then I walked toward the house. But as I opened the door, my happy demeanor faded, and I mumbled under my breath, "There is no way we're going anywhere. We have a great church, a beautiful home, lots of friends, and wonderful doctors. Alaska! That's ridiculous."

Two weeks later, I ate my words. The church board was indeed interested in Jeremy. Trying to find the joy and to be open to a new adventure from God, I decided to do a little research and at least get acquainted with Alaska. I had a gut feeling that I had been unfairly maligning our largest state—a case of Seward's Folly. There had to be misconceptions about Alaska just as there were about Louisiana. Too many people unfamiliar with the South asked the weirdest questions about Louisiana when they found out it was my home.

I'd been asked things like "Do you have an alligator as a pet?" "Do you live on a swamp?" or my personal favorite, "Do you have roads, or does everyone just get around in swamp buggies?"

My thoughts tumbled over one another. I'd heard that Alaska was beautiful, but did the sun hide for six months out of the year? And what about the snow—did it stay year-round?

I started searching on the computer. I learned that Barrow, Alaska, which was basically at the top of the world, went only three months without a sunrise and then three months without a sunset. *That's not so bad.* Fairbanks, Alaska, had temperatures that sometimes reached as high as 100 degrees. And most places did *not* have snow year-round. Wow. The pictures were amazing, my curiosity took over, and I got excited as I looked for the specific place we'd live. *Okay, surely it's someplace that has a Walmart. Right?*

Wrong.

Akutan, Alaska.

I did a search on this small island in the Aleutian chain and came up with the Alaska Volcano Observatory.

Did you read that?

V-O-L-C-A-N-O.

I walked away from the computer. *Remember, Kim, consider it pure joy, consider it pure joy, consider it pure joy . . . Okay, let's look at the facts: The island is a volcano, it's a beautiful place, it does not have a Walmart, and—did I mention?—the island is a volcano!*

That very morning, I had been studying the book of Hebrews, and wouldn't you know, the verses I chose to memorize (12:1–3) came barreling into my brain. Immediately ashamed of my selfish thoughts, I prayed, *All right, Lord, I get it. Who cares if there's no Walmart? Who cares if the island is a volcano? It will all be okay. You are in charge.*

Continuing to find the joy, I laughed out loud and asked God if dust mites could survive the cold in Alaska.

Good-bye Camry, Hello Pride

I'm completely astounded when I recall the months of change that followed my Hebrews revelation. My beautiful sister got married (another one of my crazy adventures, since I made the food, cakes, flower arrangements, and more), Kayla had to be tested by several more specialists, and we had the big Alaska decision to make.

We needed more information before making a commitment. Chuck and Diane Bundrant, the Akutan church founders and the owners of

Trident Seafoods, met with us and flew us to Alaska to visit the island. We sensed that the Lord had given us the opportunity to visit and was paving the way before us, but the decision was still difficult to make. We were happy where we were. God had given me some of the best friends of my life in that little church.

But we decided to make the jump! Things were a whirlwind after that. We gave the Akutan church our affirmative answer in May, and our house sold in three days. But we still had to sell our cars and all our furniture and then pack our personal items for Alaska. Our church friends in Louisiana were sad to see us go, but they supported our decision and affirmed that God was indeed leading us to Alaska.

But even with all the positives, several people told me I had lost my mind, and a few family members were unhappy we would willingly go so far away. Through it all, I kept telling myself that I was stepping out in faith. Because God called us, right?

There was one thing very wrong with my attitude: I was *proud* of myself for taking this leap and following God.

The comprehension of that fact hit me in the face the day I sold my car. You see, I had this beautiful, very new Toyota Camry. I loved my car. I was proud of my car. It made me feel like I was "somebody" driving that car. That beauty was the first brand-new car I'd ever owned.

The woman who wanted to buy it also loved my car. I proudly showed her all the great features and bragged about the incredible gas mileage. When she asked me why we were selling it, I again took pride in my answer that we were taking a step of faith and moving to Alaska . . . because Kayla doesn't sweat and has allergies, we wanted her to live in a cool place with no dust mites, and of course, God called us. Shoot, there was even *another* front-page newspaper article about us: "'KoolVest' Girl, Family Move to Alaska for More Normal Life."[1]

As the woman told me what a great mother I was for sacrificing every-thing to give my child a better life, I had yet another one of my two-by-four moments.

Pride was a sin.

I might have been taking a step of faith and sacrificing for my fam-ily, but I held on to my pride in so many areas. I was covering up my in-securities about this difficult move by building myself up—self-esteem turned evil. Where was my humility?

When the woman drove off in my beloved vehicle, my heart dropped. I was so upset that I had to sell it. And the evidence came swarming at me—I had a nice facade up for everyone to see. *Look at Kim. She's such a wonderful wife and mother! Just look at the sacrifices she's making.* But inside my heart was full of pride.

I walked inside the house, grabbed my Bible, and opened it to He-brews. I needed to read those verses again.

> Therefore, since we have so great a cloud of witnesses surround-ing us,

The Bible is full of these great witnesses. Witnesses who have gone be-fore us, lived their lives in faith, and been great examples to us—of the good and the bad. And we need to try to be that kind of a witness to those around us—a living testimony, shining with the light of our salva-tion through Christ.

> . . . let us also lay aside every encumbrance and the sin which so easily entangles us,

Ugh, that ugly pride.

. . . and let us run with endurance the race that is set before us,

I don't know what that race will entail in Alaska, but I'm ready to serve You, Lord.

. . . fixing our eyes on Jesus, the author and perfecter of faith,

Faith—Christ defined it. And it's what He's called us to—not something to take pride in.

. . . who for the joy set before Him endured the cross,

Did you see that? "Joy set before Him"—talk about living out James 1:2–4!

. . . despising the shame, and has sat down at the right hand of the throne of God. For consider Him who has endured such hostility by sinners against Himself, so that you will not grow weary and lose heart. (12:1–3, NASB)

I realized how petty I had become. I liked my things, my furniture, my car. But I was being asked to take a step away from that. New thoughts came to me: *Why did I care so much about a vehicle or a table and chairs? Were they of eternal value? Was I willing to endure this cross and follow Him?* God was providing the right climate and environment for Kayla. He was providing a place for us to serve. He was providing.

My Bible had a heading before those verses in Hebrews: Jesus, the Example. I prayed and asked for forgiveness, humbled and broken in my pride. Yes, He is the ultimate Example, and as I basked in His grace that day, I thanked Him again for not giving up on me.

Every Woman Needs a Friend Who Will Hit Her over the Head

We packed up all our stuff and stocked up on medications, shampoo, laundry detergent, and everything else we could think of. We would soon be leaving for Alaska, God had changed my attitude through prayer and Bible study, and I was ready. Really.

One afternoon my friend and fellow reading buddy Deanna Chang (remember my twin, separated at birth?) was helping me pack my combination office-dining-homeschool room. I gave her an area to tackle while I worked on sorting another part of the room.

Since we were both avid readers, over the years we had exchanged books and talked about our favorite, latest, great book find. During the packing process Deanna was unusually silent for a long period of time, so I lost myself in a pile of papers. A little while later, I was surrounded with designated piles for shredding, trash, and filing, when my friend came over with a thick stack of papers in her hand and promptly hit me over the head with it.

Rubbing the back of my head, I laughed and looked up at her. "Owww! What did I do?"

"You, missy,"—she pointed her finger at me—"are in trouble for not telling me."

I was really confused. "Not telling you what?"

"That you've written a book. And it's good. I glanced at it and then got completely involved in the story." She plopped the stack into my lap and stood there with her arms crossed, tapping her foot. "I'm waiting," she said. "Spill it."

Uh-oh. My friend and confidante. We had been through the wringer together. Even though we were close, I was still utterly embarrassed she had found it and actually read it.

"Um . . ." I hesitated, biting my lip. "Actually, I've never told anyone. Nobody knows. Not even Jeremy."

"Are you serious? You've never told anyone? Good grief! How long have you been writing?"

"A few years."

"Years? Girl, you've been writing that long and haven't told me?" She pointed to the stack in my lap. "Why are you hiding it? Is this book what you've been working on all this time, or is there more?"

"No. There's more." I took a deep breath and dove in. "I've always had stories in my head, but since I'm a music person, I thought it was just extra creative juice flowing, because music is what I know. Not writing. One night Josh was sick, and as I stayed up with him, I got inspired to write that story. I wrote 35,000 words that night and finished it two days later."

"You wrote this in three days?" Deanna knelt beside me and grabbed my hand. "Kim, why do you look scared to death that I found this?"

Against my wishes, tears sprang to my eyes. "Because I don't know what I'm doing! I'm a musician; I don't know how to write. I'm afraid I'll look stupid on paper."

She squeezed my hand. "Have you ever thought God might want it that way? Maybe He wants you to know you *can't* do it on your own, so that He can do it through you."

I got the message; I needed to rely on a higher power to travel a road I wasn't prepared for.

Deanna's mischievous expression was priceless. And as she stood up, I knew I was in for it.

"I'm going to make you a deal." Her tone left no room for argument. "*You* are going to keep writing, and then you're going to do something about it. *I* will in turn"—her grin told me everything—"*not* get mad at you for not telling me, and I will hold you accountable *not* to hide your light under a bushel."

Deanna had a point. She was referring to Jesus' words in Matthew 5:15: "Neither do men light a candle, and put it under a bushel" (KJV). He meant that good things shouldn't be covered up. My writing would always contain my faith—the faith that had seen us through hardship and pain—and maybe my stories would help other people understand God better. That, after all, was my goal.

Deanna went back to packing, and I sat there dumbfounded. I finally worked up the courage to ask her what was really on my mind. I swallowed. "You actually liked it?"

"Yes, you ninny! And as soon as you get settled on that island of yours, I expect to read more and hear all about what you plan to do with it."

Deanna winked at me and left me to my thoughts as she rounded up our children for lunch. I hadn't thought about hiding my light—I didn't even think this light was worth shining—but then I remembered that all my talent came from God, and that meant the light I was supposed to be shining was His. Wow. Talk about responsibility.

But why would God want *me* to write? Hadn't He given me my musical abilities? Isn't that what I should be using?

Then again, Deanna's words came back to me: *Maybe He wants you to know you can't do it on your own, so that He can do it through you.* I didn't have to feel like I had all the answers. I didn't need to do it perfectly. The more I thought about it, the more I realized He *had* used my musical talent all those years—but that was an area I had confidence in. (And I wasn't perfect at it either.) I didn't ever stress out about playing an instrument or singing in front of thousands of people. It came naturally. But what if He *did* want to stretch me, grow me, use me in a whole new area? Was I willing to put myself out there? to be vulnerable? to ask for help?

Psalm 139 came to mind; I was "fearfully and wonderfully made" for His purpose. So if I didn't know what I was doing, at least God did. And I knew that if He wanted to use the content of my writing, I needed to hand it over to Him.

As I finished packing a box, a piece of paper fluttered down from the filing cabinet. It was a quote attributed to Erma Bombeck, one of my favorite writers: "When I stand before God at the end of my life, I would hope that I would not have a single bit of talent left, and could say, 'I used everything you gave me.'"

Like I said, everyone needs a friend who will hit him or her over the head. Someone who sees your potential even when you don't have a clue as to what you are doing. Someone who loves you enough to make sure you do things well.

Deanna, Trish, and Deb—all close friends from that wonderful church in Louisiana—began to prod me along. I slowly opened up and let them read some things I was working on. Little by little I was ready to face our new world in Alaska with a new challenge: No more hiding my light. *This little light of mine, I'm gonna let it shine . . .*

Sea Lions, Foxes, and . . . Wild Cows?

In the summer of 2001, we arrived on Akutan. Forty miles east of Dutch Harbor, the small island was amazingly beautiful. A quaint Aleut village connected by boardwalks, a Trident Seafoods processing plant, and Safe Harbor Church and Community Center were all that occupied the small protected inlet. I loved it.

Though it was summer, the temperature rarely rose above 55 degrees, and so the children and I spent all kinds of time outdoors examining the wildflowers, hiking in the mountains, and learning about salmonberries and moss berries from the native Aleuts. I praised God for bringing us to such a magnificent place where the kids could play outside, and Kayla wasn't in danger of overheating. I thanked Him for educating me out of my ignorance. The kids' health improved, including Kayla's eczema, and we rejoiced.

As the months passed, we enjoyed getting to know the people of Akutan and stayed busy maintaining the large facilities of Safe Harbor. I loved taking video and pictures of the sea lions playing leapfrog, the otters waving at me with their little paws, and the pods of killer whales. The bald eagles outnumbered the humans by at least five to one, and the foxes were fun to watch from a distance. There were even wild cows on the island, which gave me more than one round of laughter. The story goes that a cattle ranch thrived on the little island decades before. I don't know why the owners left, but when they did, they left their herd—and it multiplied.

Jeremy helped teach and tutor at the Akutan School, he visited the guys working at the plant, and he played basketball with the teens each evening.

Deanna and I talked on the phone almost every day, and she was always willing to make a Walmart run for me if we needed items shipped to us. Trish, Deb, Amanda, all our Bible-study friends, and the hundreds of people praying for us in Louisiana were my encouragement and faithful e-mail companions. I continued to learn and practice the craft of writing. Little stories oozed out here and there, and my newsletters to our prayer partners were filled with humor about this Southern girl in the Land of the Midnight Sun.

Life was smooth and fun. The unpacking was done, we'd started our school year, and we were enjoying Alaska and its people, although we didn't know anyone well.

But everything changed on September 11, 2001.

The terrorist attacks that shook our nation brought us all together in prayer. We thought we were relatively safe on our little island out in the Aleutian chain, but it was scary to feel so far removed from the rest of the world.

A few weeks later an incident in Dutch Harbor would show us just how small the world truly was. A couple of al Qaeda operatives, who had allegedly been hiding on our island, were arrested. We might have been far away, in a remote part of Alaska, but the tragedy of 9/11 and the fear of terrorism was on our doorstep.

Despite the fear and devastation to our country, good came out of the disasters. We didn't take for granted the freedom we had in this great nation. And our relationships grew with the wonderful Aleut people.

Fall quickly turned into winter in Alaska, and we were given the chance to live out our faith in a very real way. We loved the people and enjoyed sharing meals and stories with them.

I baked every day and often had women over for juice, Coke, coffee, and sweets—an event they called "tea." Also, the precious children would stop by after school for apples, yogurt, and homemade bread and jam and chatter about what they learned in school.

Jeremy spent a lot of time in the village after school at the post office, chatting with the locals, letting them get to know him as the pastor in a real and normal way. The fishermen would come to the gym, weight room, and library at Safe Harbor during the week. Jeremy would let them know he was there if they needed someone to talk to, and sometimes they'd accept his invitation to come have coffee or dessert.

Akutan's weather can be severe, and most people who came from the mainland to work at the plant weren't prepared for the climate or the cabin fever they experienced. In opening up our hearts and lives to the Aleut people, Jeremy and I were able to establish a comfortable atmosphere at the Safe Harbor facilities, a homey haven for people to come to.

Ironically, the winter chill heated up an even stronger bond between Josh and Kayla. They became best friends. They rarely fought, loved playing together, and kept each other on task during school. When we lived in Louisiana, we would often stay up into the middle of the night to go to a playground, but now we had the chance to play outside in the snow during daylight hours.

We loved the snow, but it became a real challenge to get around on foot. The wind was also fierce. One day, had I not been holding the children's hands, they would have blown away, because a strong gust picked them right up off their feet.

Winter was a wonderful time, but the short hours of daylight began to take their toll.

You Are My Life, My All

After our first Christmas on Akutan, the weather turned extremely ugly. The wind was hurricane force, and since everything—phones, TV, Internet—operated by satellite, the wind blew the satellite dishes out of alignment, and we had no contact with the outside world for six weeks. Planes couldn't fly in that weather, so mail couldn't be sent or received.

One night I had a horrible headache, and by morning it was a full-blown migraine. I sobbed facedown into my pillow. I didn't understand why God would allow this pain. I thought I was doing well. And in my frustration I cried out to Him in a desperate prayer:

*Lord, I gave up everything to come to this little bitty island with no
Walmart and no restaurants and no roads. Aren't I serving You? Aren't
I doing a good job? It's just too much to take away my contact with
friends and family. I really need to talk to someone. I need to see the
sun. I need to do my Bible study with Deanna over the phone. I need
this pain to go away. I need . . .*

And then I felt that lovely two-by-four on my head again. I didn't
need anything. I was whining and complaining about what I *wanted*. A
rush of thoughts came tumbling in with the next gust of wind. In that
moment everything was clear.

I didn't *need* a car—or a road to drive it on. I didn't *need* money, or
a store to spend it in. I didn't *need* my friends or my family. I didn't *need*
to have Bible study over the phone. I didn't *need* to have contact with
anyone, I didn't *need* a roof over my head, or clothes to wear, or food
to eat.

You might say I'd lost my mind—but wait. What would happen to
me if I didn't have a car to drive? Or money? Or friends or family? The
consequences weren't so dire.

But, you might argue, what about food? And shelter?

So let me ask you this: What about food? Well, without it, I would
eventually die. But what happens after that?

And what about shelter? In Alaska, especially, I would eventually die
from exposure. But again, what happens after death? The Bible tells us
that this world is not our home—it's a passing place. A small moment in
time compared with eternity. What about eternity? It's hard for our minds
to grasp such a concept. God created us to spend eternity with Him. But
sin entered the picture. God gave us a choice, and as independent as hu-

mans like to be, we think we deserve to make our own decisions, don't we? So, we sinned. We all have. The punishment for sin is death, plain and simple. But God, in His great love for us, wanted to give us a second chance. He sent His only Son, Jesus, to die in our place, so that anyone and everyone who believes can spend eternity with Him.

Do you get my point? I had to come to the realization that the only true need I had was my relationship with Jesus Christ. Because without Him I'd be lost forever. Without His death on the cross, there is no salvation.

But *with* Him? There's eternity. Bright and beautiful, glorious and amazing.

Tears streamed down my face as His love overflowed my heart. I wasn't in control, and I didn't want to be. My priorities had once again been off-kilter. My sights had left the mark. I had veered off the racetrack onto a rocky path of my own making.

He was all I needed.

He was all anyone needed. And I was supposed to be sharing that.

My headache began to dissipate, and I pulled my guitar onto my lap. The Lord had placed a new song on my heart. A song of praise, a song of love, a song of admiration for everything He is to me.

You Are

You are my Hiding Place

You are my Source of Strength

You are my Comforter, You are

You are my Precious Treasure

You are my Joy, my Song

You are my Heart's Delight, You are

Chorus:

Age to age You have been and will be
The Alpha, Omega, Almighty King of kings
And forever, You'll reign in majesty
You are

You are my Soul's Desire
You are my Hope, my Peace
You are my Loving Father, You are

You are my Friend, my Helper
You are my Fortress Strong
You are my Firm Foundation, You are

You are my Savior
You are my Truth, my Lord
You are my Life, my All
You are[2]

Isolated Island Joy

Deanna made good on her "threats," and like the ever-encouraging, step-on-your-toes friend that she is, she bugged me about my writing. I finally decided to submit something so she wouldn't kill me. I did some research on the Internet, found the publishing house I wanted to submit to, followed the instructions, and sent in my fiction submission.

Soon afterward I received a phone call from an editor saying the transmission was garbled. She instructed me to resend the submission to a different editor via a new e-mail address. Let me fill you in on a little secret: This is not the way things are normally done in the publishing world. Editors are *way* too busy to follow up on submissions. And my manuscript wasn't that good, so why on earth did I get that phone call? (Let me fill you in on another little secret: I think God was orchestrating things on my behalf.)

Unaware of the exceptional nature of that event, I e-mailed the other editor. That little step would change my life. Over the next few months, I had many conversations with that editor, who encouraged me to keep writing. He and his wife also sent piles of helpful advice my way.

God showed me something special during that time. I was clueless about writing and getting published. Seriously. I didn't even understand the concept of writing a good synopsis or proposal. I'd never had a critique partner; I'd never been edited. But an editor told me that I had a gift, so I figured I'd better use it.

Through those unusual circumstances, the Lord blessed me in the coming years with friends, prayer warriors, critique partners, encouragers—basically in more ways than I could have ever imagined. The book you're holding in your hands is a product of years of encouragement.

In Loving Memory

I've often been asked to share with groups and churches, and after Kayla's diagnosis and the subsequent media coverage, the invitations came more often. That summer when the weather was cool enough for Kayla to travel, we'd pile in the car, stop at a church or meeting hall, share our story, and I'd sing and play the piano. More and more people began to ask if I had a CD or a book to sell. That's when a friend stepped in and said, "You need to do this." She put her money where her mouth was and donated the money for me to record a CD.

We'd always wanted to give back to the HED Foundation in some way to help other kids like Kayla. Sarah Moody and the group had donated life-changing cooling and protective equipment to families like ours who couldn't afford them. Now our family also had a way to give back to the foundation and help other kids. I would sell the CDs at my speaking events and send the profits to the HED Foundation.

The kids and I headed out of Alaska to Arkansas, where a friend donated his studio, time, and effort toward the project. With the help of a half-dozen more volunteers, who donated their time and talent to the project, the CD was recorded in three days. Now the only thing was to wait for the editing and mixing to be finished.

When I broached the subject to Sarah over the phone, she was thrilled that we wanted to help raise money. Several weeks later she sent me an e-mail telling us that she'd had cancer a few years back. She wasn't feeling well and asked us to pray for her.

The next e-mail said that her cancer had come back.

On August 8, 2002, Sarah Moody went home to be with the Lord. I was devastated. She had been a rock for me. We could talk about the most serious subjects or just be silly together—and she *always* blessed me. Kayla also loved her. She would talk to Sarah on the phone in a little-girl jabber and wanted Mrs. Sarah to see her the first time she rode a bike in her vest.

I wondered what would happen to all the families she had taken under her wing. All those people she had helped. I knew she took time for each person, as she did for me. She had an incredible way about her that made you feel loved, cherished, cared for . . . special.

And I thought about how very much I would miss her.

Sarah never had a chance to hear the finished version of the CD that included a special song inspired by her. "You'll Always Be There" wasn't for Sarah; it was for those of us left behind. It's for everyone who has a struggle or a trial, everyone who's grieving or just can't find the strength for the next day. It's a daily reminder that God is always there.

You'll Always Be There
In times of deepest grief
And when the storms of life roll in
You tell me
To cast my burdens upon You
And I know
That I am not alone

Chorus:

Every moment, every day

You're walking by my side

Even though sometimes I stray

Or try to hide

You're there

To lift me when I fall

And You're there

To answer when I call

When times are more than I can bear

I will not despair

'Cause You have promised me

That You'll always be there.

In times of darkest night

And when I cannot see Your light

You tell me

That You will never leave

And I know that I am not alone[1]

Spiritual Roots

Deanna and I had enjoyed doing several Bible studies over the phone. (And she always asked me if I needed anything from Walmart!) Each week I looked forward to our time. We would talk for a couple of hours about what we had learned, how the Lord was helping us apply it to our lives, and the humorous situations He used to get our attention.

Elizabeth George's devotional *A Woman After God's Own Heart* was one of our favorites. As Deanna and I talked one day, I had the urge to do that study again. As soon as we started rereading the study, I knew

Jeremy, Josh, and Kayla,
2 months old
May 1997

Kayla's skin turns bright
red in 75-degree heat.
June 1998

remy watches over Josh
during his first hospital
visit for acute croup.

Kayla, 18 months,
can't go outside.
November 1998

Kayla gets to be an
outside kid!
Akutan, Alaska, 2002

Kayla doesn't feel
the cold of glacial ice.
Exit Glacier, Alaska, 2004

Kim, Kayla, and Josh
Portage Glacier, Alaska, 2004

Josh and Kayla
at the Iditarod
Anchorage, Alaska, 2004

Kim and Kayla visit a church to tell their story and sing. Kayla wears the KoolVest.
Winter 2005

Kayla sick in Anchorage
February 2005

Josh, Holly Volstad, and Kayla on the day the Woodhouse family left Alaska.
June 2005

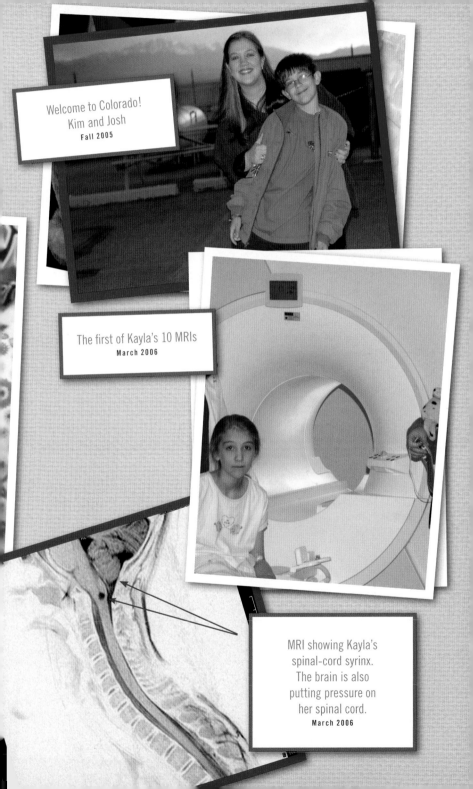

Welcome to Colorado!
Kim and Josh
Fall 2005

The first of Kayla's 10 MRIs
March 2006

MRI showing Kayla's
spinal-cord syrinx.
The brain is also
putting pressure on
her spinal cord.
March 2006

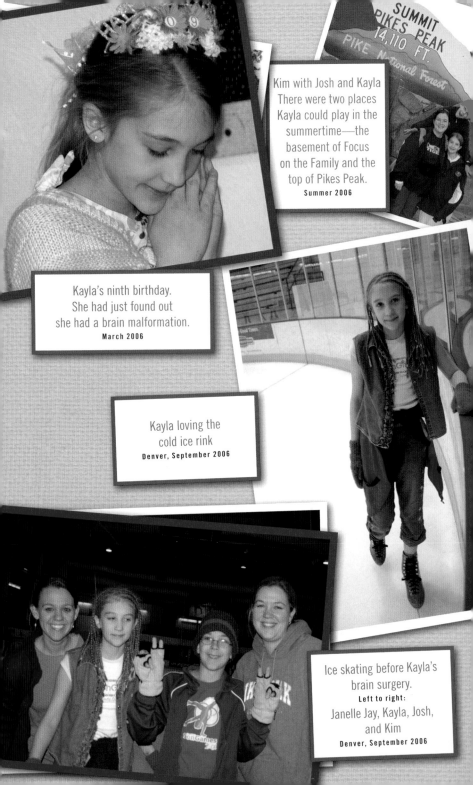

Kim with Josh and Kayla
There were two places
Kayla could play in the
summertime—the
basement of Focus
on the Family and the
top of Pikes Peak.
Summer 2006

Kayla's ninth birthday.
She had just found out
she had a brain malformation.
March 2006

Kayla loving the
cold ice rink
Denver, September 2006

Ice skating before Kayla's
brain surgery.
Left to right:
Janelle Jay, Kayla, Josh,
and Kim
Denver, September 2006

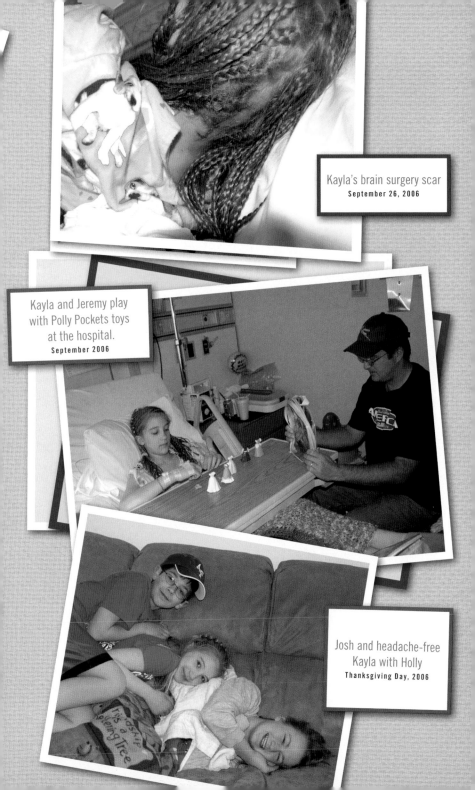

Kayla's brain surgery scar
September 26, 2006

Kayla and Jeremy play
with Polly Pockets toys
at the hospital.
September 2006

Josh and headache-free
Kayla with Holly
Thanksgiving Day, 2006

The Woodhouse Family
September 2007

MRI six months after brain surgery. The spinal-cord syrinx vanished, and the brain is no longer putting pressure on the spine.
March 27, 2007

Kayla and pediatrician Dr. Margot Crossley
February 2009

Kayla and neurologist Dr. Stephen Smith
Pueblo, Colorado, March 2009

Kayla having a pedicure
with Janelle
February 2009

Kayla and
David Phelps meet,
thanks to the Montel
Williams Show.
New York City,
February 2008

Woodhouse family
and David Phelps
New York City,
February 2008

Our welcome home.
Happy first birthday!
2008

From left to right:
Shannon Swanson, Matt Swanson (the talented builder)
with Kayla, Kim, and Josh
February 2009

From left to right:
Three men from the camera crew of Extreme Makeover: Home Edition, with Josh, Carly Grimes from the Breckenridge resort chamber, and Kayla.
Breckenridge, October 2007

PHOTO BY STEPHEN VOSLOO

Josh with author Donita K. Paul. Disney artists designed this fiberglass dragon to represent Josh's love for Donita's fantasy books, the DragonKeeper Chronicles.
March 2009

Friend Austin Healy, Josh, and Kayla on the basement bowling alley
March 2009

Kim teaches the kids in their truly extreme schoolroom.
March 2009

Josh, Kayla, and Kim make cinnamon rolls.
March 2009

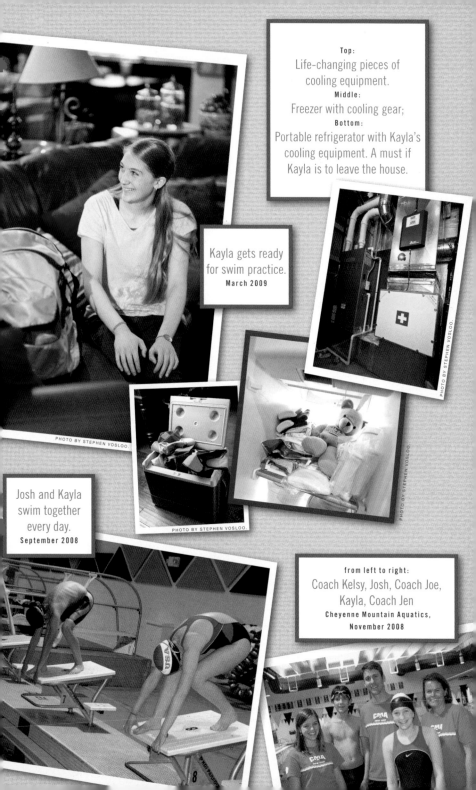

Top:
Life-changing pieces of
cooling equipment.
Middle:
Freezer with cooling gear;
Bottom:
Portable refrigerator with Kayla's
cooling equipment. A must if
Kayla is to leave the house.

Kayla gets ready
for swim practice.
March 2009

PHOTO BY STEPHEN VOSLOO.

PHOTO BY STEPHEN VOSLOO.

PHOTO BY STEPHEN VOSLOO.

Josh and Kayla
swim together
every day.
September 2008

PHOTO BY STEPHEN VOSLOO.

from left to right:
Coach Kelsy, Josh, Coach Joe,
Kayla, Coach Jen
Cheyenne Mountain Aquatics,
November 2008

8

Coach Tristan gives
Kayla pointers.
MARCH 2009

Kayla swims the
butterfly stroke.
MARCH 2009

Kayla dreams
of becoming an
Olympic swimmer.
MARCH 2009

why I felt the prodding to go through it again. I had learned so much about joy, but there were times I felt myself toppling over from the weight of my difficulties. An opening section titled "Drawing Life from God's Word" features a beautiful illustration about roots—our spiritual roots—and I realized why there were times my joy seemed to fall flat.

Roots are "unseen"—meaning our true growth in our time spent alone with God. "They are for taking in"—when we spend that time alone with our Lord. "They are for storage"—spending time in the Word and memorizing the Word gives us the foundation we need during the tough times. And "they are for support"—if we don't have a good root system, we won't hold up to the storms of life.[2]

What a powerful lesson. I had let my roots get weak. A lot of times in the ministry, the day-to-day tasks take your focus off the true goal: sharing the love of Christ and glorifying God day in and day out. Between homeschooling, taking care of my family, creating the CD project, and grieving Sarah's death, I had grown weary. I had begun to feel spiritually dry. Like I needed to be refreshed. I loved where we were. The people were great. But I tended to give more of myself than there was to give, and I was burning out. My joy was limp and withering because it didn't have the nourishment it needed.

After the 9/11 attacks, I had thought a lot about our freedom. What if our freedom to read the Bible were taken away? Would my root system be prepared? Would I have the nourishment I'd need to face the tough days ahead? Awestruck by this new revelation, I made note cards filled with little nuggets, prompts, suggestions, and keepsakes from the book about my need to "nourish up." I also made a commitment to memorize more verses, to spend more individual time reading the Bible, and to spend more time teaching my children about biblical stories and principles.

Reading Problems for Josh

Renewed by Bible studies, prayer, and close friendships, I had the energy and joy to jump back into homeschooling that fall. A few days into our routine, I noticed that Josh was having trouble with his eyes. His reading was slowing down, he would often rub his eyes while working on his papers, and headaches plagued him.

There are no doctors on Akutan. There's a small clinic, but no hospital. No pediatrician, no eye doctor. For the first time our whole family had medical insurance, but there was no way to get the help we needed without a costly flight to Anchorage. The kids had been doing so well that I'd not been concerned about this limitation before. Our prescriptions were sent by mail, and I knew there were trained personnel on the island for emergencies. *But what do I do now?*

I went to my roots. I prayed for wisdom and help for Josh. We had a couple of months before our next furlough, so I asked the Lord to take care of us until then.

When the time finally came for us to venture off our island to the lower 48, I made an appointment for Josh with an eye doctor. The doctor discovered that Josh not only needed glasses but also that the muscles of his eyes weren't working together the way they should.

She scribbled on a piece of paper. "He needs therapy. I'll set him up with a specialist here, and he'll probably need to see him once a week."

I didn't know what to say. How did I begin to explain our circumstances? "Um, that won't be possible. We live on an island in Alaska."

"Really? That's interesting." She smiled, pulled a book off her shelf, and flipped through the contents. "Well, I'll look up someone up there who can help you. Can you get to Anchorage?"

"Um, no." I had her attention now. "I can't go anywhere, the weather is too dangerous, and it's too expensive. There aren't any doctors on our island." I laughed at her reaction to my statement. "There aren't even roads, so is there something else we can do to help him?"

The doctor was clearly fascinated, and after an hour of discussion, I was armed with prescription glasses for Josh and instructions for some simple therapy we could do at home to help retrain the muscles in his eyes. She wasn't convinced it would work, but I thanked her and prayed that it would.

A "Normal" Life in the Aleutian Chain

Winter on Akutan was crazy. Snow, wind, ice, crab season—it all added up to adventure. We enjoyed being part of the community and jumped in where we could. Jeremy taught several subjects for the junior-high and high-school kids at the village school, and I taught music and preschool. There were days we would be walking through blizzards, and I would laugh as I thought of all the stories my kids could pass down about "walking half a mile to school through waist-deep snow . . ." And they wouldn't be exaggerating.

The experience of living on Akutan was one of the greatest in my life. It blessed and challenged me in so many ways. Jeremy was asked each year to "bless the boats." To do this he would have to climb on top of the crab pots and jump from vessel to vessel. He prayed for the safety of the fishermen and gave Gideon Bibles to any who wanted one. Even the hardened fishermen welcomed the prayers before they headed out to the deadly king-crab season.

I exchanged recipes with ship crew members—anything from fish and crab main dishes to carrot bread and bonbons—and spent time with the neat Aleut people. The kids played outside with the other children, watched bald eagles and whales, and helped pick berries. Kayla and Josh could have stuffed animals again, since we'd eliminated the threat of dust mites, and my heart was elated that they'd been given back this part of their childhood.

We also had the chance to meet people from all over the world and made friendships that would span the miles. Observers for the National Marine Fisheries Service taught us all kinds of cool things about salmon, cod, and the different species of whales. One of those observers, Eryn, became one of my dearest friends. As the fish seasons passed, she began to spend more time at our home after her shifts. She'd help me cook dinner, play games with the kids, critique whatever story I was working on at the time, and discuss Tolkien's Lord of the Rings with me, since we were both avid readers and fans.

Most people would never dream of living in the middle of nowhere, in between the Bering Sea and the Pacific Ocean, on a volcanic island, away from cars, stores, and restaurants. But I wouldn't have traded that time for anything.

Besides, how many people do you know who have ridden on a World War II era Grumman Goose? It's the only plane that goes to Akutan and other small islands in the Aleutian chain. It lands belly down on the water, and if you're lucky, you won't be sitting by the back door, where there are occasional leaks. No one wants to feel the trickle of frigid water on his or her seat.

I can't imagine God creating a more perfect climate for Kayla than that of Akutan. Josh and Kayla had a "normal" childhood while we were there. Remember my definition of normal? Smile. Not normal in the sense of the exotic and remote location, but normal in the sense of kids playing outside, swinging, going down a slide, riding a bike, running around. I can still see Kayla's triumphant face as she rode a bike without training wheels, ran up and down the mountains with her arms outstretched, and picked wildflowers to her heart's content. Josh loved running out the front door with his daddy, casting his fishing pole out into the bay, and watching eagles swoop down and try to steal his catch.

Leaving Our Safe Harbor

We had made a two-year commitment to the church board to stay but hoped we could stay long-term. We loved the people, and they had welcomed us into their village. The processing plant had several permanent workers who also became dear to us like family. Bea, from the laundry, and I spent many hours together discussing our next sewing projects, our Bible study, or just the kids in general. Donna had worked in the plant office for many years, and she would help us with anything we needed. All three of us loved beading and would get excited about a new pattern we had found.

I continued to write and took notes on anything I could, which resulted in files and files of story ideas. During my time teaching preschool, my little students loved for me to read to them but never let me finish a book, so I started writing my own stories to see if I could capture their attention.

I celebrated on the day when they not only listened but let me finish! I knew I had a winner when the rest of the day seemed captured by the characters. They drew pictures and asked me questions about them. The next day they'd ask me for a new story with the same characters, so the rest of the year, I worked on a children's series for my sweet little class. It was a great time in my life.

But Josh started having more issues with his eyes and developed asthma. Torn between our love for the island, which had the perfect climate for Kayla, and knowing that we needed to be closer to doctors to help Josh, we made the difficult decision to look for a new place to call home.

Within a couple of weeks, Jeremy had nine job offers. Knowing the Lord was opening doors, we purchased a pricey ticket for him to make a mad dash and visit these areas, while I stayed on Akutan and kept the church and community center running.

Traveling from Alaska to Vermont, South Dakota, Michigan, North Carolina, and several other states, Jeremy had the difficult task of finding a ministry where he fit and a location that would be suitable for our special-needs family. Not only were we looking at climate, but we were also looking for low utility costs because of our need for year-round air-conditioning, as well as close proximity to large medical facilities.

On the way home, Jeremy called me and we talked about all the opportunities in front of us. Every option seemed great, but one thing remained very clear: we loved Alaska and wanted to stay in the great state. He had a job offer at a Christian school in Anchorage, and while he was there, they drove him by some of the housing. They couldn't tell us which house would be ours, but Jeremy was confident they would take care of us. When Jeremy arrived home a few days later, we sat down, prayed, and made the decision to move to Anchorage.

CHAPTER SEVEN

Sliding Downhill

Several months later our plan for the move to Anchorage was set. Jeremy was to finish up things on Akutan, fly out to Dallas, pick up a car that had been in storage, and drive the 4,000-mile trip from Texas to Alaska. The shipping container packed with our belongings was set to be delivered sometime after my arrival.

The kids and I arrived in Anchorage on my birthday. Our plane landed late at night, and some wonderful people from Jeremy's school picked us up and dropped us off at our new home.

Now, let me make myself clear. We knew the school didn't have tons of money, and we weren't expecting five-star accommodations, but I wasn't prepared for the housing provided for us. The house was about one-third the size of the home we'd been living in. I didn't think all our boxes would fit in the house, not to mention our furniture. Adding insult to injury, the kitchen was tiny. (I love to cook, so that broke my heart.)

But the worst part was the foul smell and the wisps of fur all over the place. The previous tenants must have had at least 50 cats living there. We're all extremely allergic to cats. Happy birthday! Not. Let it be said, my attitude was not the greatest.

I hoped the fleece blankets I laid out on the floor would shield us from the allergens. But the next morning, Kayla's eyes were almost swollen shut, her eczema was out of control, and Josh was having asthma attacks.

I mumbled oh so willingly under my breath, "Consider it pure joy, consider it pure joy, consider it pure joy . . . perseverance must finish its work . . ." and called the school.

Yippee! The school principal dispatched professional carpet cleaners. I prayed for endurance. And joy.

Loading up the kids in a van the school had loaned us, we went to Walmart. We refilled prescriptions and bought cleaning supplies. I figured the carpet would need to dry, and then we could scrub the place. I pumped the kiddos and myself full of Benadryl and straightened my shoulders. Pride was an ugly thing, and I wouldn't let it stand in the way of what God was going to do. So what if I thought the kitchen was too small, or if the house was smaller than what we were used to—or what I thought we deserved. There were so many people in the world who didn't even have a roof over their heads, I shouldn't be complaining, right?

Two days later our insurance agent called and said we couldn't take out rental insurance on the property. Why? Because there was a police report that it had been broken into in the past year. More than once. Oh. Great. I hung up the phone and made sure all the doors and windows were locked. *Consider it pure joy, consider it pure joy, consider it pure joy.*

The next day I had to spend extra time in my devotions. My pride stunk. I was exhausted, and I was tired of cleaning. Kayla's eczema was worse, and Josh wasn't breathing well. I really needed to work on my attitude. I knew I was a clean freak—and yes, for good reason—but I couldn't stand the shape of the house we were in. The more I cleaned, the more layers I found that needed to be cleaned. My tendency toward being obsessively compulsive had just kicked into high gear when there was a knock at the door.

To my surprise I opened the door to two uniformed police officers standing on my front step.

"Ma'am," one of them spoke a greeting.

I just stood there. This was definitely a first for me. The only other time I'd seen policemen on my front step, I'd *invited* them because my dryer had been on fire.

"Ma'am? Can we ask you some questions?"

"Um, sure."

They wanted to know if I had seen any suspicious activity at a house not even 20 yards from mine. After the shock set in at hearing words like "crack house," "drugs," "guns," and "multiple offenses," it all became a blur. I didn't have any useful information for them, so they thanked me and left.

As soon as I closed and locked my front door, I wanted to run away. I didn't know anybody. I wasn't attached to my surroundings. (No need for snickering at that comment.) Good grief, we'd been sleeping on the floor. And I could easily call my husband and tell him it was all a mistake. We must have really misunderstood God this time. *It wouldn't be hard to pack up the suitcases. Who cares about the cleaning supplies? I'll just leave 'em.*

I closed all the blinds, locked the windows, sat on the floor, and cried.

That's it! I've had it! I can't do this! This is too hard. Kayla's getting worse, Josh is getting worse, and I've never lived in anything so icky in all my life! Lord, I don't know what You're doing, but I don't like it.

I knew I was being prideful. I was acting like a child pitching a fit, but I'd reached my limit. Glancing across the room, I saw the new Bible study by Elizabeth George I'd recently started. I got up, walked over, and picked it up off the floor. The title mocked me—*Putting on a Gentle and Quiet Spirit: 1 Peter.*

I threw the book across the room. Yep. You read that right. I. Threw. The. Book. Across. The. Room.

Now, I'm normally not one to throw things. Ever. Especially books. I love books. But as I said, I had a bad attitude.

"Putting on a gentle and quiet spirit—ha!" I blurted. "I'll show you a gentle and quiet spirit."

Immediately ashamed of my childish behavior, I heard the words of 1 Peter drift over my mind. Reluctantly I grabbed my Bible and turned to 1 Peter 1:3–9 (NASB):

> Blessed be the God and Father of our Lord Jesus Christ, who according to His great mercy has caused us to be born again to a living hope through the resurrection of Jesus Christ from the dead, (verse 3)

And I know Jesus didn't throw a book across the room when He had to face the cross.

> . . . to obtain an inheritance which is imperishable and undefiled and will not fade away, reserved in heaven for you, (verse 4)

And I don't deserve it, but thank You, Lord.

> . . . who are protected by the power of God through faith for a salvation ready to be revealed in the last time. (verse 5)

Protected? That's the problem; I feel like my security is gone. But then again, it does say "protected by the power of God through faith"— my faith. Oh, wow, oh Kim of little faith.

> . . . In this you greatly rejoice, even though now for a little while, if necessary, you have been distressed by various trials, (verse 6)

Ouch! Are you serious? How do I greatly rejoice in this . . . disgusting, too small, beneath-my-standards place?

> . . . so that the proof of your faith, being more precious than gold which
> is perishable, even though tested by fire, may be found to result in
> praise and glory and honor at the revelation of Jesus Christ; (verse 7)

My faith didn't result in praise and glory just now. I can't believe I acted that way.

> . . . and though you have not seen Him, you love Him, and though
> you do not see Him now, but believe in Him, you greatly rejoice
> with joy inexpressible and full of glory, (verse 8)

Wow. Greatly rejoice. Joy inexpressible. I need to work on that.

> . . . obtaining as the outcome of your faith the salvation of your
> souls. (verse 9)

I'm so sorry, Lord! Forgive me for my pride. Forgive me for my selfish, hateful, and prideful attitude. Help me to remember once again that I need only You.

Josh walked over to me, wrapped his arm around me, and wiped the tears off my face. Ever my sensitive, loving, compassionate child, he asked me what was wrong.

"I need more joy, Buddy. Mommy hasn't done so great in that area."

He patted my shoulder with confidence. "You've got lots of it, Mommy. God's joy." He pointed to my heart. "Right there, 'member? It doesn't go away." And with that he ran off to play with his sister.

Wow. You'd think his mother taught him that or something.

God's joy cannot be taken away. How many times had I said that? I began to laugh at my own behavior, my lack of joy.

I love it when my children remind me of lessons learned.

The phone rang, and I jumped up to answer it. It was Jeremy calling to say he was ahead of schedule. Hoping to arrive the next day, he was excited. I'd recovered from my tantrum, and I pondered whether I should try to prepare him for what he would drive up to—you know, in case his pride got in the way too. But I decided against it and prayed he would handle the situation better than I had.

Hours before Jeremy arrived the following evening, I completed the entire Bible study on 1 Peter. For extra credit I went through my concordance and looked up every reference for "joy" and "rejoice." Noting that the book of Philippians had 16 references to those words, I ordered a Philippians in-depth study by phone from Precept Ministries. I couldn't wait for it to come. I needed to keep reading the Bible; I needed to hold on to God's joy—even in the ickiness around me.

Jeremy drove the 4,000 miles from Texas to Alaska in less than four days. A long-time, close friend from Louisiana, Daniel McCabe, made the trip with him to make sure he stayed awake. I didn't want to know how they did it, but I was thankful they both made it safe and sound.

As soon as they arrived, my husband walked into our house and asked how I was doing. As he looked around, his jaw tightened, and I could see the hurt on his face. This wasn't what he'd been expecting either. I think we were both thankful that Daniel had come. Laughing with a friend over the situation was much better than pitching a fit.

I squeezed Jeremy's hand and told him it would be okay. There was no need to tell him what it took me to get to this point of optimism. It would only hurt him more. I took a deep breath and went back to cleaning. Daniel asked what he could do to help, so I gave him the job of scrubbing the cabinets and laying down shelf paper. I couldn't have given him a better job—Daniel has an engineering degree. I have never had more perfectly laid shelf coverings in my life.

Cat-Infested Carpet

Several days later we unloaded the shipping container, rented a storage unit for everything that wasn't a necessity, and attempted to joyfully settle into our new abode. But I worried about the kids' health. Kayla's allergic reactions had gotten so bad, she was mutilating herself again in her sleep. And I had helped Josh use an inhaler many times to keep his asthma in check. Finally I drove up to the school, met Tammy Vachris, one of the nurses, and asked her for advice about a good pediatrician.

God gave me a special gift when He put Tammy into my life. Not only would she become a good friend, she would be a huge help with the children's special needs.

Tammy and I talked a long time that day about Kayla's issues and Josh's asthma. She told me about a pediatrician she greatly respected and knew well because his kids attended the school. I was elated, and armed with his contact information, I headed home.

Dr. Stephen Baker examined Josh and Kayla the next day. The kids immediately liked him, and I knew we'd found a winner. But Dr. Baker was seriously concerned about Kayla. I gave him copies of all the medical files on her and told him I'd already started her on a round of antibiotics because she was so susceptible to staph infections.

After nine weeks of different antibiotics, Kayla's skin was still in horrible shape. All the medication had done was keep the infections at bay, but without eliminating the cause of the flare-ups, there was no hope for healing. I felt like a terrible mom for not being able to help my little girl, and Jeremy took it very hard that Kayla wasn't doing well in our new home.

Dr. Baker went to the school and asked them if they could do anything about our housing. Particularly the carpet. We had a bagless HEPA vacuum, and cleaning just the living room would fill up the canister. The carpet was still full of cat hair, dander, and dirt. One day I vacuumed the same 10-by-10 square of carpet over and over and filled the canister nine times. And remember, this was *after* the carpets had been professionally cleaned. But I kept grabbing on to God's joy and continued to vacuum over and over again.

Dr. Baker knew the house was making the kids too sick, and he was afraid for them. But the school couldn't afford to fix any of the problems, so we waited for other housing to become available.

One day one of the houses on our street was being partially demolished and rebuilt. I looked out the window toward the heavy machinery and saw a sight that completely grossed me out. Thousands of mice (shrews) were running from underneath the debris. And they were running toward *my* house, their long tails wriggling. I screamed. Yes, screamed. And then I climbed on top of the couch, watching the floor as if I knew at any moment the army of rodents would find their way inside.

And just in case any of you are wondering, I don't do mice. Can't stand them. Think they're disgusting. *Panic mode* is too wimpy a phrase to use in describing my frame of mind at that time. I started bleaching everything. They weren't inside yet, but I just knew they were coming. I imagined the skittering noises all those tiny feet would make, and I went through the house getting everything off the floor as high as I could. I told the children to stay on their beds, and they watched me with confusion on their little faces as I moved quickly through the house.

Jeremy arrived home a little later to find everything stacked on top of tables and bookshelves as high as it could go. He approached me with a question in his eyes, but before he could speak, I blurted out, "We've got to move." Then I explained what had happened.

My husband, knowing my need for cleanliness, laughed. He put his arms around me and told me he understood, but what were we supposed to do? He attempted to joke about it to help me see the humor in the situation. And then, as the wonderful husband that he is, he went to the store and bought the entire stock of mousetraps. Just in case.

In the meantime, I was offered a job teaching music at the school. I was torn between my love of teaching and wanting to be available for my children. As a family we decided to enroll the children at the school, and then we could all be together if I decided to teach as well.

Our family was once again without insurance, and Jeremy and I were worried about taking care of the kids' medical needs. Private insurance companies shied away from us because of Kayla's diagnosis—the first word in that diagnosis being the dreaded *hereditary*. But after investigating thoroughly, we found a wonderful state health-care plan for lower-income families. Ecstatic over the news, we applied, and waited.

After several months Kayla's health went steadily downhill. We needed to move, but we were stuck. There was no way we could afford the housing prices in Anchorage.

"The Light Fixture Tried to Kill Me!"

A few weeks into the academic year I decided to teach up at the school as a substitute, and I enjoyed being around the students, my husband, and my children. After praying about it, Jeremy and I decided I would take a permanent position at the school, and maybe, just maybe, we'd be able to afford to buy a cleaner and safer place to live. I put my writing aside, thinking it was a dream that would need to be fulfilled later, and poured my heart into teaching music again.

Jeremy loved teaching Bible, and the students adored him. Parents would catch up with him just to say that their child loved Mr. Woodhouse's Bible class. Serving as pastor at churches and camps all those years before had been wonderful, but Jeremy loved the interaction with his students just as much. I'd always loved teaching as well, and this school and the students held a special place in my heart. We relished getting to know the kids and interacting with them. We knew we'd made the right decision.

The extra income from my job helped us qualify for a home loan. Mary Stephens, our chosen Realtor, had a tough assignment: to find an affordable house that would provide a healthy environment for Josh and Kayla.

Mary became like family. She studied my notes about Kayla to the point where she could almost tell Kayla's story as well as I could. And, wow, was she diligent in her work. Her checklist went something like this: Never had pets inside? Air-conditioning? No mice? Never had smokers inside? (Kayla and Josh were both highly allergic to smoke.) Inexpensive? No drug dealers next door? She wouldn't take us to a house until she'd investigated it, and eventually she found a winner. It was brand-new.

The day we closed on the house, we were all excited. Kayla came to me that morning with a great idea. We all had fun with the secret project, and when we went to Mary's office later that afternoon to celebrate, we handed her a framed certificate that made her an honorary Woodhouse Family Member. Mary cried as she held my two beautiful children, and I told her I would never forget what she sacrificed to find us a safe place to live.

Have I mentioned that if something's going to happen, it's going to happen to Kim?

The week we moved into our new home, we also emptied the storage unit. I made headway unpacking—even to the point of making a path to the children's bathroom so they could actually take a bath. Wow. I know, progress.

After Kayla had taken a bath upstairs, Jeremy was draining the water while I creamed her skin. Josh was next in line for a bath. I walked into the kitchen, which was downstairs, to get a glass of water for Kayla, when a large explosion-like sound above my head made me jump back. Before I knew what was happening, the entire four-foot fluorescent light fixture that had once beautifully adorned my kitchen ceiling crashed around my feet, surrounded by a giant waterfall.

I didn't move for several moments as water soaked into my socks and I stared at the pieces on the floor.

Jeremy ran down the stairs and, eyeing the mess, asked, "What did you do?"

"I didn't do anything. I have no idea. I was getting a glass of water, and then the light fixture tried to kill me."

Jeremy chuckled at my attempt at humor and then suddenly gasped as he realized where the water was coming from. He ran upstairs to plug the drain in the kids' bathtub, asking me to phone the builder as he ran.

The builder came to inspect the damage immediately. He discovered that the drain to the children's bathtub hadn't been sealed. When the bathtub drained, it leaked and filled up the small space between the tub and the kitchen ceiling. Once that was full, it started draining through the little holes around the wiring for the kitchen light, and then it filled up the light fixture. It was really a pretty casing, but it wasn't capable of holding a bathtub-sized amount of water. Thus, the explosion and subsequent crash.

Once again I reminded myself to consider it joy. So the ceiling and insulation had some water damage. It could all be fixed, right? No one was hurt, and we had another bathroom.

While Jeremy talked with the builder about the plans for the repairs, I sneaked upstairs and pulled out my Philippians study. One of my favorite features of those in-depth studies is the fact that I have to do the research myself. No one else did the homework for me; there were no commentaries, no helpful headings in text. As I studied each verse, each section, each chapter, I filled in the blanks for myself about what the Lord had taught me. I flipped the pages in my notebook to find my "At a Glance" chart and reviewed the chapter themes as I'd labeled them going through Paul's letter.

- Philippians 1—Joy in circumstances, no matter what!
- Philippians 2—Joy—Be like Christ; follow His example
- Philippians 3—Joy—My goal for life: rejoice in the Lord!
- Philippians 4—Joy defeats all worry

Can you see a pattern? It's pretty clear what the Lord had been working on in my life.

I smiled, sitting there with my ginormous notebook in my lap. Jeremy came up the stairs and asked me about my silly grin.

"Joy, honey. It's all joy."

The Amazing Alaskan Mainland

Akutan is amazing, but the great state of Alaska has a lot more to offer than the Aleutian chain, and we enjoyed discovering the magnificent mainland. There were so many places to go, so many things to see. And you could *drive*—real cars on actual roads.

One Sunday after church we drove the Seward Highway down to the Exit Glacier. That drive is one of the most beautiful in the world. Awed by God's amazing creation, Jeremy and I talked about our journey. Not the journey we were on in our vehicle, but the journey of our lives. We'd been through so much in our short 12 years of marriage and had learned some hard lessons, and yet we still had a long way to go. The roller coaster, with its twists and turns, had been bumpy, to say the least. But as we talked we knew the Lord had brought us through storms to make us even stronger and to make our marriage even better.

That day seemed to signify so much more than just an outing as a family. We'd made a lot of mistakes along the way. We weren't perfect, but love and forgiveness have the ability to give you a fresh start each and every day. As we absorbed the majestic wonder of God's handiwork, we were refreshed and saw the newness and splendor of His love and grace.

Just like tourists, we'd get excited every time we saw a moose or a bear, or the great mountain Denali off in the distance. And every time I saw moose "nuggets," I'd stand and look at the mound in amazement that an animal of such enormous stature could produce such perfectly shaped piles of . . . um . . . poo. The kids and I loved to hike trails, and Josh and Kayla would yell, "Hey, Mama! There's another pile of nuggets here. You wanna take a picture?" Yes, I must admit I took many shots of those superlatively formed pellets. If you've ever seen them, you've probably taken a picture too—just 'fess up.

Even with all the glory of Alaska around me, I still missed Akutan. I missed the quiet, the lapping of the waves, the wind blowing 5,000 miles an hour and knocking you off your feet. I missed the abundance of eagles on our island. And I missed the people. A lot.

But I was thankful for the medical care Josh and Kayla were receiving.

Josh's glasses were helping his eyes, and a specialist sent us a new vision-therapy computer program for him to use. He would work with the program for a few weeks, and then he would see the specialist again to check his progress. Our new insurance didn't cover the in-office therapy, so the specialist tried to keep the number of office visits to a minimum, and we prayed for Josh's eyes to strengthen.

Life moved on at a rapid pace. We loved our new house, but even more, we loved our students. Josh and Kayla were doing fantastic in school, even though they both expressed that they missed the amount of time we used to have together. We'd always had *all* our time together, so it was an adjustment for each of us. But even though our schedules were hectic, I tried to see the kids at least twice every day at the school.

Kayla had to see the nurse several times a day to put the prescription cream on her hands. Then she'd wear little cotton gloves back to class. Tammy, the nurse, took great care of our sweet girl.

Everything seemed to be running smoothly. Everyone had notes about Kayla's condition and paid close attention for any warning signs—even slight changes in skin coloring. One day at school, Kayla looked a little "too pink" for the PE teacher, Mrs. Dyson. So she immediately took Kayla to the nurse, and then they went outside in the *freezing* cold. Kayla be-bopped around in the snow in her short sleeves and cooling vest as if nothing was wrong, while poor Mrs. Dyson stood beside her in her shorts and T-shirt. Mrs. Dyson relayed the story to me a little later, and I couldn't help but laugh with her as she reenacted how she stood shivering in the cold, waiting for Kayla to cool off. That neat PE teacher earned a great deal of respect from me that day. The fact that she was watching and did the best she could to keep my child safe meant the world.

So Very Far Away

Several weeks after Christmas, my friend Deanna called with devastating news. Her younger son, two-year-old Jonathan, had leukemia.

Remember, Deanna had been there for me through everything. She supported me, encouraged me, prayed for me. My heart cried out to the Lord. I felt useless. I couldn't be there for her and didn't know what to do. But I could pray.

As I fell to my knees and prayed, Kayla came into our room, followed by Josh. We all held hands in the middle of the floor and prayed for our precious friends who lived so very far away. Deanna's older two kids were very close to Josh and Kayla, and I knew my sweet children were feeling the heartache as well.

As Jonathan fought for his life in the hospital, the lessons in joy that I had learned took on a new depth of meaning. The kids and I spent more time in prayer for each other and for the Chang family. My soul ached for Jonathan's healing.

A Summer Filled with Gifts, Trials, and Surgery

As Jeremy taught Bible and I taught individual voice and piano lessons at the school, our relationships with the students in Anchorage grew deep. We knew the Lord had brought us there for those kids, and we loved being a part of their lives. The church we attended was large, with a huge music department, and I enjoyed being involved in the ministry there.

We also invited people to our home for a small-group Bible study. We shared a meal each Friday evening with Kelly and Chris Heitstuman, Curtis and Leah Patteson, and Eryn Kahler. Jeremy would lead us in our study, and we all grew spiritually and as friends.

Josh's therapy had helped his eyes by leaps and bounds, and each time we saw the therapist, his sessions were shortened. He no longer had to use the computer program, and soon he was released from therapy.

But as the school year wore on, I noticed that Kayla had clammed up. She wasn't excited about school anymore and wouldn't tell us what was wrong.

Summer arrived, and we traveled around the lower 48 states. Time and distance gave Kayla perspective, and she finally opened up about the events at school. A girl in Kayla's class had said some ugly things to Kayla about her skin sometime after Christmas. Once we were out of Alaska, Kayla felt comfortable talking about what had happened. Each time I'd talked to my kids about gossip and not having nice things to say, she had obviously listened, because she didn't want to tell me in case it would get the other child in trouble. I was amazed at the maturity of my seven-year-old.

As the story unfolded, my heart broke for my little one. Apparently, that one child's comments had made all the other kids think that something was wrong with Kayla, that she had something contagious and really yucky.

We had a long talk about Psalm 139 and how we are created special. But Kayla was still convinced she didn't want to go back to school, saying, "I just want to be homeschooled again, Mama."

Now, we love homeschooling and had made the decision to homeschool in Louisiana and Akutan because it was the best thing we could do for our kids. After two years in an isolated area, though, we thought it would be great for the kids to attend this Christian school that took precautions for Kayla and didn't mind chilling out a classroom so she could be a part of the group. Especially since my teaching there allowed us to afford a clean, safe home.

But I didn't want Kayla to think that schools are bad because some children say mean things, intentionally or not. I told her we needed to pray about it and ask God to direct us to the correct decision. Wanting to do what was best for my kids, I knew I'd stay home again in a heartbeat. But I also worried how that would affect us financially. I reminded myself that God knew best. He knew what we were going through. He loved us and knew our needs. I would leave it in His hands.

Our road trip finally brought us to Deanna's house. I watched her lovingly care for her children and saw her heart in her eyes. Even though I'd faced a good many medical emergencies, I couldn't imagine enduring what she was going through with her young child, but I was so thankful for the chance to finally be there with her. While we were there, little Jonathan had many treatments and shots, but Deanna held together in an amazing way. The long road to healing that lay ahead of them seemed daunting, but she faced it with a strong determination. My heart broke when I had to leave and head back to Alaska, but I was refreshed by our visit and so thankful for the precious time.

After our summer trip, we returned home to Anchorage. I received the wonderful news that one of my best friends, Leah Patteson, would be teaching Kayla's grade. I talked to the principal, Leah, and Kayla. I knew Kayla adored Mrs. Patteson, that she would feel comfortable in Mrs. Patteson's class, and that Leah would go to great lengths to ensure that Kayla's health was not at risk.

In August Josh's glasses prescription needed to be changed. I'd noticed that a birthmark above his eye had begun to grow, so we asked our wonderful ophthalmologist, Dr. Davis, to check it out.

Josh had a linear sebaceous nevus. What had appeared as a birthmark above his eye was actually a growth that had the potential to be cancerous.

After Dr. Davis explained this anomaly, he suggested surgery to remove it, since it was growing and in such close proximity to Josh's eye.

Once again I found myself in a doctor's office, wondering about yet another thing to add to our list of medical issues. Poor Josh! He'd already had surgery to correct his breathing problems and had undergone therapy for his eyes. He was a constant encouragement in our struggles with Kayla's neurological disorder, and now this.

As Dr. Davis left the room, Josh scooted close to me and hugged me tightly. I smiled down into his big brown eyes and told him we would need to hang on to our joy. He giggled as I tickled his sides and asked him if he had his joy.

He smiled up at me and said, "If Kayla can go through all her stuff, then so can I, Mama. I've got my joy."

We talked a little longer and came up with some new questions for Dr. Davis. Josh asked him to make sure that he was really asleep before cutting around his eye. The kind doctor laughed at Josh's joke, assuring him he would do just that.

Josh's linear sebaceous nevus was removed in August, and he healed remarkably fast. Kayla and Josh began to get excited about school again, and as another school year started, we all settled into our routines.

Tongue Inspection

My schedule was so full, I had to start teaching private lessons at 7:30 AM— well before school actually started—to accommodate everyone. Jeremy had a busy teaching and coaching schedule, and Josh and Kayla were enjoying their new classes.

The fall colors were incredible in Alaska, but you had to pay attention so you didn't miss them before winter descended. Most of our time was spent either at school or church, and time seemed to pass too swiftly. We were blessed with so many wonderful students and friends. Many of our "kids" would spend time at our house on the weekends, and we continued to host the Friday-night Bible study in our home with close friends.

The fall of 2004 was also full of doctors' appointments. Our neurologist wanted us to meet with a team of geneticists who flew in from Seattle. We met with one doctor for more than an hour and a half. He stated, "She looks so normal. She's such a beautiful child."

I chuckled inwardly and thought, *Now where have I heard that before?*

I explained to him about the word *normal* and how it had a different definition in my life. He just looked at me as if I'd lost my mind.

He continued his thoughtful evaluation and questioning, so fascinated with Kayla that he had to prove to himself that she actually had HSAN. His amazement grew as Kayla didn't respond to pinching, poking, and scratching, which should have registered as "ouch." But the confirmation for this doctor came when he stood Josh and Kayla next to each other and had them stick out their tongues.

The fascinated doctor pulled my arm to draw me closer so that I could inspect my children's tongues. "See here, Mom? Kayla clearly has half the fungiform papillae her brother has."

"Huh?" Shaking my head, I tried to form a more intelligent reply. "I mean, I have no idea what fungiform papillae are. Please explain."

"*Fungiform*, meaning mushroom-shaped. *Papillae*, meaning nodules."

Yep, that cleared it up. My brows scrunched in that "are you sure you know what you're talking about" stance on my forehead.

Obviously noting my lack of confidence in his explanation, he continued, "They house taste buds. Your daughter has half as many as your son."

I finally understood what he was saying, and I thought back to all the times Kayla had said that something was too spicy or too sour. But the baffling part was that there were times when I thought something was really intense, and she didn't. I asked the geneticist about it, and he told me that there wouldn't necessarily be consistency with her. It was also a new confirmation of her diagnosis, and that was another big piece of news for us all. The geneticist said the information might help doctors care for our daughter in the future.

My Worst Nightmare Comes True

Christmas passed in a flurry of outings, get-togethers, school programs, and church musicals. January hit hard with more snow and extreme low temperatures. We had just settled back into our regular routine when a series of unfortunate events sent our world into chaos.

I don't know exactly what happened, but Kayla's teacher was absent one day, and a substitute teacher took her place. That morning the thermostat was raised in the classroom, and soon Kayla was asking to go see the nurse about her skin. The nursing staff noticed that she didn't look like her normal perky self, but they sent her back to class anyway. Several hours later Kayla told the teacher her head hurt. The substitute sent her to the nurse's station. My friend Tammy had left the school for a new position, and so Kayla was met with a new staff member—and a crazy number of sick children who had beat her to the nurse's station. When the nurse took Kayla's temperature, it didn't sink in that it was too high. She sent her back to class.

Another hour or so passed, and Kayla turned pink and glassy-eyed. The substitute teacher knew something wasn't right but didn't understand Kayla's condition. She sent Kayla once again to the nurse, but the nurse's office was still jam-packed. This time Kayla's face said everything, and the nurse called me, upset and apologetic that she hadn't seen it before.

They brought her immediately to my room, and I knew as soon as I saw her. Kayla was burning up with fever.

CHAPTER EIGHT

Joy in the Darkness

Kayla lay down on the floor of my room until they could find someone to teach the rest of my classes and students. The longer she was there, the tighter a ball she curled into, and the less responsive she became.

My heart dropped as her temperature slowly crept up, and I called Dr. Baker. I hoped it was just a virus of some sort, but a fever could be deadly for Kayla if it couldn't be kept under control. We all carried that worry in the back of our minds.

Days passed. Kayla's temperature wouldn't come down, and she was lethargic, almost lifeless. When she did speak, she complained that her head hurt, and that's what worried us the most. Up to that point Kayla had never actually said that anything hurt. She'd never had a stomachache, never had a headache, never had *any ache* of any kind.

The more I thought about it, the more my insides twisted into knots. She doesn't feel pain until it's 20 to 30 times the intensity.

How much pain was she in for it to register as "hurt" to Kayla?

Dr. Baker spent days doing tests, taking blood, and treating our precious baby in his clinic. I think it was almost as hard for him to see Kayla in that condition as it was for our family. Several times during our appointments, I caught him praying. He would look up with the slight sheen of tears in his eyes, and I knew—this was serious. (At this point we couldn't hospitalize her because there was no way to cool down a room.)

He called every night for an update and instructed Jeremy and me to keep meticulous notes on her temperature and pain levels throughout each day.

When Kayla's headaches and elevated temperature lingered for more than two weeks, I took a leave of absence from my job at the school. I had to stay with Kayla; she was the priority. I couldn't continue to teach when we had no clue what was wrong with her or how long this would go on. My heart ached to relieve her pain, and yet there was nothing I could do.

I called Deanna to check on Jonathan's progress with his fight against leukemia. He had relapsed in December, and I knew that she would understand my emotional pain like no one else. Her friendship had blessed me like no other. As we shared the burdens of our hearts with each other, we prayed for our families. Their doctors were working to get Jonathan into remission again so they could perform a bone-marrow transplant. Our doctors were trying to find the cause of Kayla's serious condition. Our hearts were so heavy during this frightening time, but we tried to encourage each other even through the darkest of days.

Big Bear

Near the end of January, Kayla had her first CT scan. I told her we would go to Walmart afterward and get something for her as a treat, since they had to poke her once again to put in an IV for "contrast." (It's not very sensitive to say "dye" in a hospital.) Kayla had developed an aversion to needles ever since she awoke in the middle of the nerve-conduction study. Of course, if I had awakened to a bunch of steel pins sticking out of my body, I'd probably have issues with needles too. Wouldn't you?

By the conclusion of the scan, I knew that Kayla had hit another low. She wrapped her arms around my waist just to make it to the door. My feet felt as if they weighed 500 pounds each as I held back the tears and walked her slowly, carefully out of the testing room. A nurse brought a wheelchair for me to help Kayla out to the car. I walked behind Kayla as I released my emotions and wept.

Josh held Kayla's hand as I wheeled the chair out to the parking lot. I lifted her into our vehicle and buckled her in. Leaning my head back, I closed my eyes and prayed. *Lord, give me strength. This is more than I can handle—but I know that You can handle it.*

Sweet Josh kept talking to Kayla and asked her what she wanted from Walmart. I didn't think she would make it through a trip to the store, and I assumed we would just go home, but I heard her tiny voice say, "Can I have a new teddy bear, Mama?"

Turning the vehicle around, I drove straight to Walmart.

Josh helped me get a shopping cart. I laid a pillow in the bottom and hefted my seven-year-old into it. She curled up into a little ball again but didn't completely shut down yet. "Mama, it hurts."

"I know, sweetie, I know. I'm so sorry it hurts."

"But we're gonna consider it joy, right?"

"Right, baby. Consider it joy." I was so choked up, I couldn't get anything else out. Here she was in incredible pain, and she was reminding *me* to rejoice. Wow.

Kayla didn't say another word, and looking down at her, I knew that her headache had intensified.

I looked at Josh and smiled, attempting to ease the worry so clear on his young face. "Okay, buddy, I need your help. We are going to find the biggest and bestest, most cuddliest teddy bear we can find, all right?"

Josh cheered up when I gave him a job. He told me he knew it was important to help an adult with stuffed animals, because we didn't always know how to pick the best one. I giggled and nodded in agreement as we headed for the toy section.

And wouldn't you know? We didn't need to go that far. Valentine's Day displays were up, and there were aisles completely filled with stuffed animals. And on the end of one display sat the largest, squishiest, softest stuffed bear I had ever seen. Josh grabbed the bear's paw and dragged it off the shelf. As he wobbled back and forth with the bear, he called out to Kayla, "How's this one?"

Kayla opened her eyes and offered the tiniest of smiles. It was enough to make me want to buy 20 of those bears. She held that bear in her lap all the way home. He was huge, at least four feet tall, with a head at least three times the size of Kayla's. When we arrived at our house, she took the bear to the couch and lay down on top of him. She named him Big Bear.

Big Bear became part of the family. He was Kayla's comfort, her pillow, her best pretend friend. We couldn't go anywhere without him. And she did her best to hold on to him and smile—even in the worst of pain.

The Long Haul

Kayla went through several lumbar punctures (aka spinal taps), CT scans, and emergency-room visits. Nurses drew vials and vials of blood out of her veins for just about every test in the book. They tried prescription medications for migraines and numerous other conditions. She couldn't have an MRI without being sedated, and that was too risky.

It had been six long weeks of headaches and elevated temperatures. The journal for Kayla was filled with thermometer readings, labeled with times and levels of pain. Nothing gave us answers, and no medication seemed to help. Flipping through the journal pages, I cried out to the Lord.

Father, I'm tired. Thank You for sustaining me and holding us all in Your hands through this trial. But please, please, help us find what is causing this horrific pain in Kayla. And if that isn't Your will at this time, give us the patience and strength to keep on.

I held on to my joy, but I was weak. It was hard, and I felt exhaustion pulling me down. I gave notice at the school because we didn't know if Kayla would get better the next day or six months down the road, or . . . I didn't want to think about the alternative.

Late one night when I couldn't sleep, I climbed out of bed, trying not to disturb Jeremy, and pulled on my robe. As I passed a bookshelf on the way out of our room, a title caught my eye: *Three Steps Forward, Two Steps Back*. My heart felt that way—every time we made progress with Kayla's condition, we had a setback. My anguish inside grew as I watched my listless child day after day.

I pulled the book off the shelf and went downstairs.

After I poured myself a glass of water, I grabbed my Bible and Chuck Swindoll's book, turned on the gas fireplace, and curled up on the couch. *Please, Lord, I need some encouragement.*

I opened up the book and looked at the table of contents. Having read the book before, I scanned for something that would reach out and grab me.

Chapter 6 did it: "Waiting: Lingering Test of Patience."

I devoured the chapter quickly. My dad has known Chuck Swindoll for a long time. When I was growing up, our whole family always listened to his tapes in the car, so I could hear Chuck's voice reverberating in my head as I read, laughed, cried, and then gasped. Guess which verses he talked about at the end of the chapter? James 1:2–4. This is what Chuck wrote:

> Let me remind you of what I told you at the beginning of this book.
> The key word is *perseverance*. We grow and we learn—not when things
> come our way instantly—but when we are forced to wait. That's when
> God tempers and seasons us, making us mellow and mature.[1]

It was so comforting to read about perseverance once again. To know that I wasn't the only one who struggled. I wasn't the only one to go through difficult circumstances. I wasn't the only one who got impatient. I reminded myself of everything Deanna had endured through Jonathan's illness and prayed for my sweet friend.

Reciting James 1:2–4 several times to myself, tears ran down my cheeks. His joy was still there. He hadn't taken it away. But maybe I had lost my grip on it a little. Maybe I'd gotten distracted by the hardships of life and wanted to handle that burden all on my own.

I hopped around to different chapters in Swindoll's great book and pored over favorite passages in my Bible. Then I decided to go back to 1 Peter and read that incredible letter. You see, a lot of people think of the book of 1 Peter and are immediately reminded of suffering, because the passage talks a lot about it. But I remembered that the point of 1 Peter isn't just about suffering or warning us we're going to go through suffering. It's about how we, in turn, deal with that suffering.

How was I going to react to this difficult time in my life? That question resounded in my brain over and over. I read through 1 Peter to help me make a conscious decision.

> In this you greatly rejoice, even though now for a little while, if necessary, you have been distressed by various trials, (1:6, NASB)

I will rejoice, Lord. I will rejoice.

> . . . so that the proof of your faith, being more precious than gold which is perishable, even though tested by fire, may be found to result in praise and glory and honor at the revelation of Jesus Christ; (1:7)

I am so weak, Lord—but I want people to see You through this. I want them to see Your joy and Your love.

. . . and though you have not seen Him, you love Him, and though you do not see Him now, but believe in Him, you greatly rejoice with joy inexpressible and full of glory. (1:8)

I will rejoice, Lord. I will rejoice.

Beloved, do not be surprised at the fiery ordeal among you, which comes upon you for your testing, as though some strange thing were happening to you; (4:12)

Your strength is perfect, and I will rely on You.

. . . but to the degree that you share the sufferings of Christ, keep on rejoicing, so that also at the revelation of His glory you may rejoice with exultation. (4:13)

I will keep on rejoicing, Lord. I will rejoice.

The next morning I awoke refreshed, even though I'd had very little sleep. I was grabbing on to God's joy, and I was determined not to let go of it again. Trials and grief are a very real part of life. Suffering would come; there would be many hardships and a lot of tears. But the point?

Do not despair.

I knew I needed to talk to Kayla. There were several times I had broken down and cried because she was in so much pain that she couldn't respond or focus. She didn't need to feel bad or take the blame for making Mama sad. So I went to her room and sat on the bed beside her. She was obviously in a lot of pain, but she reached out to hold my hand. I told her how much I loved her, that she wasn't the one who made me cry. I cried because I hurt for her. Moms are like that; we don't want to see our babies in pain. I also explained my decision the night before.

As soon as I said the words "I will rejoice," Kayla perked up ever so slightly.

"You mean, like the song we wrote?" she whispered in a quiet voice.

It took a moment for me to understand what she was saying, but then I knew exactly what she was talking about. Several years before, Kayla had helped me write a song titled "Hallelujah."

Hallelujah
I will rejoice
I will give thanks
I'll lift my voice in praise
I will rejoice
I will give thanks
I'll lift my voice in praise

Chorus:
Singin' Hallelujah to our God
Glory and honor to the Lamb
Singin' Hallelujah, praise His name
His love for all let us proclaim
Hallelujah, Hallelujah, Hallelu-Hallelujah
Singin' Hallelujah, Hallelujah, Hallelu-Hallelujah

Let creation shout for joy
Let the children clap their hands

Let us all cry out in praise
In wonder of His amazing grace[2]

The words are simple and repetitive—but exactly what needed to be said. I told Kayla that if either one of us got down, we were going to remind each other to rejoice, to consider it joy, to persevere, no matter what.

God knew what He was doing. He had a plan for our lives.

Even in her pain, Kayla sang our song softly to me until she went back to sleep.

Just Keep Swimming

Kayla's muscles tightened up when she was in pain, and it worried me to feel the stiffness in her body. Especially when she was in the fetal position for the majority of the day and night. I would try to stretch her out, but I realized that curling up was probably the only way for her to deal with the pain. Dr. Baker knew Kayla loved the water, and swimming was good exercise for her, so I asked him if he recommended pool therapy. He snapped his fingers and told me that just might be the answer. Not only could we try to move Kayla's muscles, but the water would help bring her temperature down. So he prescribed that Kayla swim at least an hour every day.

After the trial run at a local club, with great benefit to Kayla, a friend donated a pool membership so Kayla could get in the water every day. Each morning after I dropped Josh off at school, Kayla and I would head to the pool. Kayla barely moved or spoke, but I would drag her in the water for lap after lap until her body would loosen up and she would move on her own. Those hours in the pool were such an encouragement to me. To see Kayla actually liven back up was good for my heart. And if we could have just stayed in the water all day, every day, we would have.

Several weeks later we were all exhausted from tests, swimming, and still no answers. Josh came home from school with the flu, and then I got sick. During those days, we all pretty much lay on the couch together. One afternoon Josh asked if he could homeschool again. He wanted to be with us and said he would rather homeschool again anyway. I was attempting to homeschool Kayla as much as I could, but most of the time, she couldn't even sit up, much less do schoolwork.

Josh was my little social guy. He'd never met a stranger, even when he was a baby. I was shocked at his request, as we had thought we'd just let him finish out the school year. We talked about it and prayed about it; Josh was sincere in his desire and decision. When Jeremy came home, I shed tears when I told him that my precious boy wanted to be with Kayla and me all day.

After prayer and some more heart-to-heart chats with Josh, we decided to bring him home as well. It ended up being a huge encouragement to Kayla, and to Josh as well. I didn't realize how much worry he was carrying around at school, wondering how his little sister was faring. He helped me ease Kayla into the water each day and cheered her on. He would hold her hand for each doctor's appointment and encouraged her to keep trying—no matter what.

Dr. Baker continued searching for answers and spoke with our neurologist about some other medications to try. One drug was especially heavy duty. Before the doctors would allow Kayla to take the medication, she would need an electrocardiogram (EKG) to check her heart. Both doctors meticulously went over details with us so that we would be ready. They asked us several intense questions. Did we want to go this route? Were we prepared for side effects?

We made the decision to give the medication a try, hoping that something would bring Kayla relief. The EKG went well, and Kayla began taking the prescribed pills. The doctors thought it would take about six weeks for it to truly start working, so we settled in for another long wait.

During these weeks I had a few students who came to my house for their private piano and voice lessons. It was hard on all of them to see Kayla curled into a ball, glassy-eyed and unresponsive. Most students tried to get Kayla to talk or play a game with them, and their concern and compassion touched me deeply. No one wanted to see her in that condition. Several of the kids left our house in tears, but they always came back convinced they could do something to cheer Kayla up or help in some way. My students grew incredibly close to our family, and the bonds remain to this day.

One particular afternoon stands out in my mind because of a very special and remarkable young man—Andrew Hall. Andrew was hanging out with the kids while I taught lessons to teens Joanna and Holly. Kayla lay curled up in a ball on the couch, holding tight to Big Bear. The girls both had voice lessons that afternoon, and as the time progressed, Kayla worsened. When Joanna's lesson finished, she reluctantly told me she needed to return home. Waving her good-byes to all of us, she kissed Kayla on the head and told her to keep her chin up. Andrew sat on the floor in front of Kayla, playing a board game with Josh. The full-of-life young man—strong and hardworking—was headed for the navy. But within his muscled and solid exterior beat a soft heart for children. Kayla had formed an attachment to him, looking up to Andrew like an uncle. That afternoon would prove to be an incredible hurdle for Andrew as he watched one of his favorite little people fade into her pain-filled, glassy-eyed, almost-lifeless state.

The door closed abruptly, and Holly came up the stairs for her lesson with tears in her eyes. "I think Andrew is really hurting for Kayla right now. He needed to leave for a few minutes."

Holly worked hard on her piece for state competition, but I could tell her heart was aching. Andrew returned 20 minutes later, out of breath, and his cheeks tear-stained. He'd obviously taken all of his frustrations and anxiety out in a hard run.

"Mrs. Woodhouse, I'm so sorry I left."

Stunned by the depth of my own emotion over this incredible teen's maturity, I brought him some water. "Andrew, it's okay. This is hard on all of us. I'm just thankful that you took the time to be here."

"Well, I need to explain. I was overwhelmed by the sight of Kayla and the amount of pain she must be in. It crushed me to think that she was hurting. I needed to talk with God about my frustration watching her suffer."

I simply nodded at him and smiled. I understood completely. Some people handled it with tears, some with anger or questions, and some needed to run all out until their lungs were bursting as they pounded the pavement in pain.

Andrew walked back into the living room and knelt in front of Kayla. "Hey, little princess. I'm back."

Kayla looked up at him with the slightest glimmer of a smile. "Hi, Andrew."

Within the hour Kayla's pain level shot up. She called to me and asked if she could go to bed. She simply couldn't take it anymore. Andrew put his hand on my shoulder, walked over to the couch, and scooped up Kayla and Big Bear. He knew it was quite the feat for me to carry her and her favorite stuffed animal up the stairs at the same time.

She buried her head next to his as he carried her all the way to her room.

That precious picture will stick out in my mind forever. Andrew ex-uded strength, youth, and the readiness to take on the world, yet he carried little Kayla like she was a porcelain doll. It reminded me of Jesus carrying a little, injured lamb with great care and gentleness.

On days when Kayla's pain was the worst, I would have to place my hands on either side of her face and force her to focus on me and respond. Josh would often sit on the floor in front of the couch and read books to her. He was so worried about her. His love and fierce devotion to his sister were evident every day in his care for her.

Kayla's and Josh's birthdays were fast approaching, and I prayed every day that she would have a good day and be up and around. She really wanted to have a party, and so did Josh. The headaches were so regular that most of the time they blurred from one right into another. I had no idea how to pull off a celebration. But I planned a party anyway and invited a few of their friends. Many of our students and several other teachers wanted to come as well. I asked everyone to be prepared, though, just in case it was a bad day, which most of them were.

On the day of the party, we headed out to the pool. I was hoping I could keep Kayla in the water long enough to help her feel better, and maybe she could enjoy at least part of the fun before another headache hit.

That morning Kayla truly came alive in the water. I saw glimpses of her former self and wanted to cry with the relief of it. And as we swam, she sang the song like the beautiful blue, yet absentminded, fish Dory from Disney's film *Finding Nemo*: "When life gets you down, ya know what you gotta do? Just keep swimming. Just keep swimming. Just keep swimming, swimming, swimming!"[3]

We laughed at the appropriateness of the music and continued to sing. We swam and swam until I realized that if we didn't leave, we'd be late getting home for the birthday bash. I prayed the whole way home that Kayla would remain at least partially headache free—enough to allow her to enjoy a small part of the celebration.

The Lord answered my prayers that beautiful spring afternoon. Kayla was alert, smiling, talking, and had no headache for almost the entire day.

Kayla and Josh's love for swimming grew by leaps and bounds. There was an older gentleman who swam every day in the lane next to us, and we found out one day that he was a retired Olympic swim coach. Over time we learned each other's stories, and he gave me pointers on what to teach the kids. One morning he stopped me during our workout and asked the kiddos to keep on swimming. He looked me in the eye and told me that Kayla had serious potential and that I should encourage her to keep going. I was a little baffled at his declaration because the kids had never had lessons, but I thanked him for his insight. He wrote me a list of books that I could read and reminded me that he was there if I ever had any questions.

That coach's input was incredibly useful, as the kids and I needed to be in the water every day, and sometimes I wasn't sure what to work on next. Through it all, the coach had amazing patience for all my questions and always had a word of encouragement for the kids. His kind prompting about Kayla's future stuck in my mind, and I wondered what we could do to indeed provide a bright future for Kayla and Josh.

To Stay or Not to Stay

Four months passed, and Dr. Baker was concerned that Kayla's issue was bigger than any of us realized. He knew we wanted to stay in Alaska, but he also knew that Kayla's condition was extremely rare. To properly treat her, we would probably have to make many trips to specialized hospitals.

Jeremy and I prayed and prayed about what the Lord would have us do. Should we consider moving back to the lower 48? And if we did, where would we go? The South was too hot, but at least everyone, including stores and restaurants, had air-conditioning. The North was cold, which was good, but most states still get way too hot for Kayla in the summer, and the majority of homes and other places didn't have air-conditioning. The other consideration was her extreme allergy to dust mites. In Alaska it was cold and dry, and we didn't have any problems. But moving to another climate that might have higher humidity and warmth would make dealing with the nasty little allergens a nuisance again.

An opportunity for ministry in Colorado came up, and after a lot of prayer, we decided to visit Colorado Springs. I was concerned about traveling with Kayla, since she was still plagued with headaches, but we wanted to see how she would do in the elevation over 6,000 feet.

The trip was an amazing success—the entire week we were in Colorado Springs, she didn't have one headache. But it was still heart wrenching to think of moving away from our beloved Alaska.

Several more job offers came to Jeremy over the next couple of weeks. Some were in the lower 48, and others were in Anchorage. Jeremy loved his teaching position and his students, but with Kayla's unknown malady hanging over our heads, it wasn't possible for me to work. We needed to be able to survive on Jeremy's income alone, but with the low pay of his teaching job, it wasn't possible to provide a healthy home for Kayla.

One question remained: What was best for Kayla's health?

And the only way to find the answer was to pray.

Kayla finally started getting relief from the headaches, and her temperature leveled off to a regular reading. Another EKG showed that her heart hadn't been affected by the intense medication. Dr. Baker hoped the medicine was finally doing its job—after nine weeks—but he still didn't know the cause of Kayla's illness. The headaches were obviously a symptom of something else. Our beautiful little girl was still not back to "normal," but we prayed she was on the mend.

Feeling the Lord leading us to Colorado, we made the incredibly hard decision to leave Alaska. We knew we needed to be closer to specialists.

It took more than three hours just to fly from Anchorage to Seattle, and that was only going to the northwest part of the country. If we needed to fly to the East Coast or to one of the Mayo clinics, it would take even more travel time. But the thought of leaving our close friends, students, beloved doctors, and the amazing state that was truly home just about ripped our hearts out.

A lot of our students came over to help us pack and spend the last few weeks with us. So many fun things took place—Courtney and Lindsey overflowing the sink with soap bubbles, Joanna and Holly singing with Big Bear as their dance partner, Kayla's giggles filling the room as she was entertained by music students. Josh loved being in the middle of the chaos, telling everyone his latest story or showing off his latest LEGO invention. His relief that Kayla was doing better was apparent to everyone around as he allowed himself to enjoy all the love and fun surrounding him.

My sister, Mary, came to visit and help me pack. Each time we moved she was there, ready to help me do my inventory and load the boxes. And in between all the work, we tried to venture out and get a few last glimpses of our amazing Alaska.

Two short weeks before we were scheduled to leave for Colorado, a couple of "kids" from our youth group in Arkansas—Mandi and Jennifer McCann—came to visit and help us pack as well. They had been a huge part of our lives when Kayla was diagnosed with HSAN. They had babysat my children and were as close as family to us. Adults now, and both of them RNs, they helped me do more research on Kayla's odd illness. One day we were discussing some things in a medical journal when I received a phone call from Deanna.

She was relieved. It had been three months since Jonathan's bone-marrow transplant, and he was doing incredibly well. The doctor was encouraged and cleared him to run around and be a kid.

We were all ecstatic with the news.

Then our joy was crushed. A couple of days later, Deanna called again. Jonathan had relapsed. The leukemia was so aggressive and so far spread, the doctors didn't think he had long to live. Our conversation was short. My dear friend needed to spend every moment she had holding her precious son and her family.

Jonathan Craig Gwo-Ty Chang went home to be with the Lord not even a week later.

My heart felt as though it had broken in two. Jonathan had fought the disease so valiantly. I had begun to breathe the fresh air of hope for my friends, but the jolt of the shock felt as if all the air had been sucked out of the room.

So much sorrow and grief! *Lord, this seems to be too much to bear! Please be with them. Wrap them in Your love and strength. Give them comfort as only You can.*

Jeremy, Josh, and Kayla were devastated when I broke the news. Our families had been close—the children were all very close. A dreary fog threatened to overtake me. I still had packing to do. I still had to leave Alaska. But my best friend had just lost her child. I couldn't do anything to help her. I couldn't get there for the funeral. I couldn't bring that feisty, rambunctious, and full-of-love toddler back.

CHAPTER NINE

When the World Falls Apart . . . Don't Quit

In June of 2005 we spent many days saying our good-byes to friends and then began the amazing journey down the Alaska-Canadian (ALCAN) Highway toward what we hoped would be a new future for Kayla and Josh.

Our wonderful Realtor in Alaska, Mary Stephens, sold our house in a few weeks. By the time we left Anchorage, everything was in her capable hands and taken care of. A company in Anchorage had donated air-conditioning equipment for our family, so while the rest of our belongings were taking the long sea route to the lower 48, we pulled a U-Haul trailer behind our truck. That trailer was loaded with what we needed to survive until the shipping container arrived and the life-saving equipment was ready to be installed in our new house.

We had an amazing family time driving down the ALCAN Highway. It was a healing journey. There were moose, bears, eagles, mountains, lakes, glaciers, wildflowers, mosquitoes as big as small birds, and a "sign forest," just to name a few. We took our time stopping, taking pictures, and just being together. Jeremy patiently and considerately stopped almost every 20 feet because the kids and I would want to take a picture of something else new and interesting. But my favorite memory is actually of *Jeremy* with the camera.

We spotted a couple of black bear cubs. After Jeremy pulled over, I couldn't get out of the truck because of the muck and mire on my side. So he took off with my camera. This was a big deal because Jeremy normally couldn't care less about pictures—of anything. But this time was different. He was like a little kid, sneaking over to snatch a glimpse of the baby bears playing. I watched him in the side mirror, laughing at his antics until he came barreling back to the truck, holding my camera way over his head. Yanking his door open, he jumped in the driver's seat with greater speed than I had seen him use in many years—especially with his bad knees. Before I could even voice my question, he looked at me and explained that mama bear had all of a sudden shown up, and she wasn't happy that he wanted to play with her children. We all had a good laugh at his story, but when Jeremy looked in the rearview mirror, there was mama bear in the middle of the road, coming after us. Thankfully, my husband's reflexes are quick, and we drove away.

It was a trip none of us will likely ever forget—a good time for us to grieve for our friends, and for all those we left behind, and yet look forward to our new life in Colorado.

Our Realtor in Colorado Springs, John Unzueta, had done a great job helping us find a home that fit our needs and our budget. We were excited about our new house, had a company on call to install the AC as soon as we arrived, and were ready to unpack and settle in.

Twelve long days on the road were taking their toll. We were tired of hotel beds and weary of sitting in the car, and I was looking forward to making a home-cooked meal. Finally arriving in Colorado Springs, we drove up to our house, and Jeremy and I got out of the car.

One itty-bitty problem: No one was around when we showed up. The builder was surprisingly absent, the house wasn't finished, and on top of that, the place was a wreck. We had picked out colors for paint, and none of that was done. An upstairs bathroom was supposed to be a full bath, and it wasn't. There were coffee stains on the brand-new carpet and a hole in one wall, along with significant hail damage along the back of the house. Poor John looked at us and apologized; the builder had said it was done. The last time John had visited, the house had been in good shape. We walked around the house as we tried to decide what to do.

With the shape the house was in, it needed a good several weeks' worth of hard work to finish and clean up. Our biggest issue was a safe and cool place for Kayla, since it was summertime. Most houses in Colorado Springs were sold without air-conditioning, thus the need to install it as soon as we moved in.

Jeremy was not happy. Remember, he's very black and white. If you tell him you're going to do something, you'd better do it. The fact that the builder was nowhere to be found and the house wasn't ready to move into added up to Jeremy feeling like he had been lied to.

My sweet husband walked over to me and put his arm around my shoulder. "Are you okay?"

I wasn't sure how to respond at first. You know us women, we have that need to nest and make a home, and more than that, I was seriously concerned about living arrangements for Kayla.

Jeremy must have sensed my indecision. "It's going to be all right. We'll find a house. We can't buy this one . . . I'm sorry."

I laughed. "You mean we're homeless?"

I think my hubby must have felt some relief that at least I was laughing. "Yeah, we're homeless. But let's try to fix that, okay?"

Home Again, Home Again . . .

It was still early in the day when I walked out onto the beautiful front porch of the home that would not be mine. The kids were inside the air-conditioned vehicle watching a movie, and I waved at them. Jeremy and John were in the house discussing paperwork, and I preferred not to listen to all the reasons *why* the builder was in breach of contract. I just knew I had wanted that house. I'd already configured the organization of each kitchen cabinet, and I had mentally slotted the placement of each piece of furniture. My favorite part of this house from the pictures had been the porch; it spanned the entire front of the house and had an incredible view of Pikes Peak. Alone, I stood there for a few minutes, praying for strength and wisdom.

Feeling a little lost, I muttered, "Consider it pure joy, consider it pure joy . . ."

"What'd you say?" John asked as he walked out onto the porch.

I laughed. "Nothing, really. Just mumbling to myself." I didn't want to admit how difficult this really was for me. Trying to keep the joke going, I told John that we were homeless, and I had never been homeless before.

He looked very concerned. I guessed that my jovial facade hadn't worked, and he must have known I was struggling.

"We'll find a house for you guys, Kim. Don't worry."

John made some calls, reserved us a hotel room for later that night, and the search began.

I'm sure we made quite the sight, driving around from neighborhood to neighborhood in a truck covered in mud and bug guts from our 12-day road trip, pulling a large trailer.

After looking for several hours, we took deep breaths, as we had to come to terms with a big problem. The housing market had climbed dramatically during the summer months, and we would have to pay a lot more for a house than we'd anticipated. And houses were in high demand; one house rose in price by more than $20,000 in a mere 30 minutes, supposedly because of price increases and upgrades that weren't originally listed. And three different people wanted to buy it! We were shocked.

Jeremy again tried to soothe my concern, "Honey, don't worry, I'll get a second job if I have to. And since Kayla is doing a little better, you'll be able to teach lessons again. We'll figure out how to make it work."

Later that evening we wound our way through John's neighborhood, where they were still building a new section. They had a house ready that was beautiful and had enough rooms for us. All the rooms were relatively small, but it was the cheapest house we had found that could accommodate all of our needs. We made an offer immediately, afraid we would lose yet another home before the end of the day.

As night descended we left the builder's office. John breathed a dramatic sigh of relief, and Jeremy and I laughed. We did it. We bought a house. Now we just had to wait for our bank to redo all the paperwork for the new purchase and close the deal so we could move in.

After almost five weeks of living in hotels from Alaska to Colorado, the papers were signed, and we moved into our new home.

God's timing is always perfect, and I was reminded once again of the fact when we received a call the next day telling us that our shipping container would be arriving.

Breakthrough Headache

The rest of the summer passed with unpacking and settling in. Some good friends of ours had been in a horrible car accident in Montana, and

Jeremy went to help them for a week. After he returned, the kids and I headed to Deanna's to spend some much-needed time with our friends in Texas.

By the time we returned home, it was time for our homeschool year to begin. But I still had a lot of junk to deal with in the garage. A sweet lady from our church, Jacque Nethken, came over with her children, Garrett and Brandi, one day to help. She brought food for dinner, and we worked in the garage all day long. The children had a blast together, and Jacque and I formed a bond that would be the beginning of a wonderful friendship.

We started school, and time seemed to fly by. The kids loved home-schooling, and I felt blessed more and more each day by their sweet spirits and genuine eagerness to learn. Josh was doing really well, his eye muscles had retrained, and his asthma was under control. Jeremy loved his work, we'd made incredible friends, and Kayla's health seemed to be okay.

Until one horrific day in October.

We were out buying a freezer when Kayla became very clingy and quiet. The trip wasn't a long one because we had already picked out the appliance we wanted, but I noticed Kayla going downhill.

Kayla leaned hard against me. "My head hurts. Really bad."

My heart sank. I didn't want to believe it was happening again. Had I forgotten her medication? Was she becoming immune to the pills?

The interior of the car was strangely silent as we drove home. Dinner was also more quiet than usual, although Josh did his very best to try to cheer Kayla up.

Halfway through the meal, Kayla looked up at me with glassy eyes and pleaded, "Mama, can I please just go to bed. It hurts."

I nodded at Jeremy as I choked back the tears and walked with Kayla upstairs to her room. She clung to Big Bear and squeezed her eyes tightly shut. I prayed with her and asked God to give her rest and to please ease her pain. Kissing her cheek, I told her to let me know if she needed anything.

The stairs seemed to have five times the number of steps on the way down. I kept telling myself to hold it together, that it wouldn't do any good to lose it. I didn't have the appetite to finish my meal, so I just started cleaning up. Josh and Jeremy were solemn as they brought me their plates. They also must have lost the desire for food, as most of it looked untouched.

Jeremy took Josh upstairs, helped him with a math page, and then tucked him into bed.

I stood at the sink washing the same pot over and over. Grief overwhelmed me, my knees buckled, and I slid to a crouched position on the floor. As sobs wracked my body, I cried out to the Lord, *Why? I don't understand. Please help me to understand.*

Jeremy heard my sniffles but couldn't see me crouched behind the counter. He came into the kitchen, found me, and asked what was wrong.

"Nobody here knows," I threw at him through my tears. "Nobody here has seen it. They've heard about her disorder, and they've heard about what happened in Alaska, but they don't *know*! At least in Alaska, I had a support system, all those people who went through it with us. They saw it with their own eyes, they prayed for Kayla, they hurt for Kayla, they all felt the anguish seeing her lifeless and unresponsive."

Jeremy nodded. "And you're afraid no one will understand. You're afraid of having to explain it over and over again. You're afraid to let people in because it just hurts too much."

I pulled my knees up to my chest and cried into my hands.

"God knows," Jeremy continued, "and I know. I don't understand why Kayla is going through this again any more than you do, and I don't know what God's plan is, but we're going to keep going. We *have* to keep going."

Jeremy grabbed my hand and pulled me to my feet into a fierce hug. We had fought many battles over the years. We had climbed many mountains, only to find it to be the first step of many. And we had prayed.

Life was never easy. Jeremy was right; we *had* to keep going.

The next morning Kayla's headache was miraculously gone. I called our phenomenal new pediatrician, Dr. Margot Crossley, anyway. She asked to see Kayla the next day and help figure out what had happened. And hopefully she could find some answers to prevent it from happening again.

I gave the kids an art project to work on so I could spend a little more time pulling myself together. My devotions that morning had been brief, and I needed encouragement.

As I opened my Bible to Philippians, I went to chapter one, verse six: "He who began a good work in you will carry it on to completion until the day of Christ Jesus." A story came to mind that told of the famous Polish pianist Ignace Jan Paderewski.

According to the tale, Paderewski was scheduled to perform at a great concert hall. A mother had brought her young son to hear the talented musician that night. As the child grew impatient waiting for the concert to begin, he wandered up to the shiny, black grand piano on the stage and began to play chopsticks.

The audience quieted at the sound of the simple tune but soon turned on the young boy, yelling for him to get off the stage. Paderewski heard the commotion and walked onto the stage behind the boy. As the master musician began to play a counter-melody and accompaniment with the small student, he whispered in his ear, "Don't quit. Keep playing. Don't quit."

I remembered that Chuck Swindoll wrote about this same story in the introduction of his book *The Finishing Touch*. I went to the bookshelf and pulled it down, opening to the beginning. Swindoll wrote a poignant reminder to us all:

> We hammer away at life, and sometimes it seems about as significant as "Chop Sticks." Then, about the time we are ready to give up, along comes the Master, who leans over and whispers: "Don't quit. Keep going," as He prods His finishing touch of grace, love, and joy at just the right moment.[1]

I opened my Bible to Philippians and read the whole book—*twice*. Sometimes I marvel at why God puts up with me. How many times do I need to be reminded of His goodness, His love, His grace, His *joy*? But I love to hear Him ever so gently say, "Don't quit, Kim. Keep going. I've got it under control." *He who began a good work in me . . .*

At our appointment the next day, Dr. Margot (as she prefers us to call her) checked into everything she could think of. She and Dr. Baker agreed that the headaches were merely a symptom of the ultimate cause. She knew it was time to dig a little deeper. Kayla needed an MRI.

Of course, there was one small hurdle to jump: we had no insurance.

When we first moved to Colorado—wanting to be honest—I had let the insurance in Alaska know that we moved out of state and immediately applied for the state insurance in Colorado. But for some strange reason, our applications never went through. The paperwork got lost over and over, someone would make a simple clerical mistake, and I would have to apply again.

This wasn't the first of our medical woes changing states. I'd had more than 20 different doctors turn down the care of my daughter because it would "take too much time," "take too much research," or it was "out of my realm of knowledge."

To complicate matters even more, Kayla's prescriptions ran as high as $1,500 a week. Her skin was still having horrible eczema issues, and one little tube of cream was $160. We could go through sometimes two in a day, and that was using it sparsely, trying to make every drop count. And that was only *one* of her creams.

Dr. Margot labeled the migraine from the day before as a "breakthrough headache," meaning that it broke through the barriers of the medication. We had originally hoped to wean Kayla off the meds, but after what had happened, Dr. Margot didn't think it was wise.

And so we waited.

For answers. For insurance. And for a green light to finally have the much-needed MRI.

One Letter Changes Everything

We all loved living in Colorado—we had learned to live in joy and find the good everywhere we moved. The people were great, the views spectacular, and the elevation had proven beneficial for all of us. We had a generous donor who paid for our membership to the YMCA so the kids could swim, and there we met Erica Duval. I saw Erica across the pool wearing Louisiana State University flip-flops one day, and so I wandered over to say hello. Over time we became close friends, and she also became the kids' first swim teacher.

Another wonderful person had bought us a family pass for the Pikes Peak Highway, which wound 19 miles up to the summit of "America's Mountain." Kayla and Josh loved to get all their schoolwork done so we could take a "field trip" up Pikes Peak for a picnic. After several phone calls, the rangers recognized my voice as I called to check the temperature and weather at the top. One wonderful man would always say, "It's perfect Kayla weather today, ma'am. Come on up!"

Thanksgiving, Christmas, and New Year's passed in a flurry of fun activities and get-togethers with good friends. By the time January arrived, I had applied 11 times for the kids' insurance. I talked to Jeremy about taking out a loan to pay for the MRI, feeling defeated and worried about Kayla's health. She was getting clumsier and had lost some color. The headaches hadn't returned, but I was concerned that the medication was taking its toll on her.

January was a tough month on Kayla's skin. Her feet seemed to be bearing the brunt of it this time. She'd always had bad cracks on her heels from as far back as we could remember, but we were fighting infections once again. I felt like we were on a merry-go-round, going in circles. We'd tried everything but never could get the cracks to heal. Dr. Margot came up with all kinds of great ideas, but we still didn't have any success. One visit she finally looked up at me and laughed.

"Have we ever tried a pedicure?" Dr. Margot said slowly as if still thinking it through. "We'd have to find the right person who understood her condition so they wouldn't inadvertently hurt her, but maybe . . . just maybe that might work."

I could hear the excitement in her voice build as she talked about her idea. Caught up in the thrill of a possible remedy, I thought it was worth a shot until reality brought me firmly back to terra firma. "How often will she need to have it done? Aren't they expensive?"

"Well," Dr. Margot said, taking the blunt approach, "it's either try this or have Kayla lose the tissue on the bottom of her feet because it's so damaged."

"Okay, then." Blunt obviously worked. "Let's try it." I tried to think positive. I wondered if they gave loans at the bank for long-term salon needs.

My friend Chris and her husband, Kelly, had moved down to Colorado from Alaska that month. Since she knew so much of our history, I called her on the way home from the doctor. Laughing, I explained the situation—and told her I needed help. I had no idea where to start looking.

Chris laughed hysterically at my loan idea, but she knew that we would have to figure something out. We prayed together, and I went home to make some phone calls. I had to start somewhere.

An hour later Chris called me back. She was so excited, I couldn't understand a word she was saying.

"Chris, start over. I didn't get any of that."

"You're not going to believe where I'm at!"

"Okay, where?"

"I'm outside Starbucks."

I didn't understand the significance of her being at Starbucks, other than the fact that Chris needed coffee to breathe.

"I just met the coolest lady. Wanna take a guess at what she does?"

I was definitely at a loss for words but didn't have a chance to guess.

Chris's words spilled out so rapidly, I had a hard time keeping up. "She works at a salon, silly! She's a nail tech, and we were talking while we were in line. I told her all about Kayla and what the doctor said. She said she'd love to work on Kayla's feet—and guess what? She wants to help out for free!"

"Wow." It took several minutes for all the information to sink in. "Are you serious? You met her at a coffee shop? And she just happens to do this for a living?"

"Yep."

"Wow. God is so cool."

The next day Janelle Lucas came to meet us. She took us to look for products she could use on Kayla that wouldn't give her an allergic reaction, and by the end of the week, Kayla had her first pedicure.

Dr. Margot also recommended switching to organic foods and non-chemical cleaners because Kayla's allergies were so severe. Her eczema would flare, the itch would be intense, Kayla would scratch and destroy her own skin, and then we'd have to fight off another infection. During the day it was relatively easy to keep Kayla from scratching. If I told her to stop, she would stop, most of the time not even realizing she was scratching. But nighttime was a different story. Even with gloves on, she would tear through her skin in her sleep and never know.

Everyone was constantly on the lookout for a way to prevent the flare-ups from ever happening. We'd started out gradually with milk from a wonderful local dairy, Royal Crest. When we began to see a difference, we found a man who was a butcher, and he purchased us an organic cow for our meat. Thankfully the organic foods were available in our area, but the cost wasn't going to be easy to swallow. We all noticed Kayla's skin improve but knew we couldn't afford to triple our grocery budget.

Chris started bringing over staple foods that were organic to help us out, and I have a feeling she was the one to spread the word, because soon we were finding gift cards to Whole Foods in the mail, in the milk box on our front porch, and taped to the front door.

It was during this time that Kayla began to overheat in even cooler temperatures. It became so severe that we finally had to lower the house temp to 62 degrees. While we had all acclimated to 65, it took us awhile to not feel frozen in our house. I learned to just keep moving. And we all wore sweatshirts—except Kayla.

Late February blew in with a snowstorm—and a letter.

We finally had confirmation: the kids would be covered by insurance. Kayla could have the MRI.

Dr. Margot called our neurologist, who then scheduled the MRI. Two weeks later we sat in the waiting room of the radiology department.

Children Kayla's age are normally sedated so they can't move during the scan and it will come out clear. The nurses all looked at me strangely that first time I told them Kayla could not be sedated. It took a good 20 minutes of explanation for them to realize that it wasn't a *desire* for her not to be sedated; it was a medical necessity. Since our discovery during the nerve-conduction study, I knew it wasn't wise to attempt to sedate Kayla, have them start the scan, and then her jerk to wakefulness in the middle, ruining the test. I made a mental note to thank Dr. Edgar for giving us that nugget of wisdom. I had no idea how important it would be to let people know that she didn't react well to the medical procedure.

The next day I journeyed to the store with the kiddos to refill prescriptions. Kayla's eczema was flaring up again. Thankfully it wasn't a warm day, and Kayla had her vest on. But we weren't planning on being in the store very long anyway. I picked up a few other necessary items as the pharmacist finished filling our order. My cell phone jangled in my pocket, and I answered the call.

"Hello?"

"Mrs. Woodhouse? This is Dr. Morgan."

Relief filled my voice. "Yes, ma'am. I've been looking forward to your call. Do we have any answers?"

"Mrs. Woodhouse, are you sitting down?" Dr. Morgan's voice was very calm.

"Um, no, actually I'm picking up prescriptions." I began to feel uneasy. "Please just tell me."

"First, let me tell you that what we found was quite unexpected. We do have answers." Dr. Morgan cleared her throat. "Kayla has another very rare condition. I believe it was what caused the migraines."

I held my breath and whispered, "Please . . . go on."

"Kayla has a brain malformation called a Chiari malformation of the brain. And there is a syrinx that has developed in the spinal cord."

I sat down on the floor of the store. The words were stuck in my throat. How did I respond to that? I didn't even know what it meant, but it sure didn't sound good.

"Mrs. Woodhouse?"

I croaked, "Yes . . ."

"Let me explain." She sighed heavily. "Kayla's brain is being squished by her skull. Since the brain doesn't have enough room, it is basically oozing down into the top of the spinal cavity. The brain is then putting pressure on the spinal cord, which I believe caused the syrinx to form. The syrinx is what we believe to be a fluid-filled cyst. Although it is irregularly shaped. It could be something else."

"And you think this is the cause of her headaches?"

Dr. Morgan was quiet for several moments. "I am truly hoping that this is the cause." Another deep sigh. "But I have to warn you that this malformation has also been with Kayla since birth, so there are several things we must consider. One is the fact that the syrinx may not be a syrinx after all—it could very well be a hole. If it is a hole, it could have caused her nerve disorder and may never go away."

The fog of shock was beginning to lift, and I was able to wrap my mind around what the doctor had just told me. "I'm assuming this has to be corrected, and it won't be easy?"

"If it's as bad as we think, Kayla will need brain surgery. Because she doesn't feel pain like other children, it is very risky to wait until she is symptomatic. The neurosurgeon has already seen the MRI and would like to see Kayla as soon as possible. Your appointment is tentatively scheduled for Monday."

Monday? That's only four days away. Oh, my. The seriousness of the situation bore down on me like the proverbial ton of bricks. We had waited in the past for three or four months to see specialists. And this one already had us on the schedule in four days.

I finally found my tongue. "Thank you, Dr. Morgan. I need to go home and find my husband so that he'll know."

As we hung up, I somehow peeled myself off the floor, wheeled the cart around, picked up the prescriptions, and loaded the car.

Brain surgery? My poor baby. How is she going to take this news?

And then in the back of my mind the words repeated: consider it pure joy, consider it pure joy, consider it pure joy, consider it pure joy . . .

I felt the Master's touch that afternoon driving home. He told me to keep going and not to quit. That even then, distressed by a trial, I could rejoice with joy inexpressible and full of glory.

I didn't know how. But I knew I could.

CHAPTER TEN

The Brain Is an Amazing Thing

Monday came before I was ready for it. Jacque came and sat with Josh while Jeremy, Kayla, and I headed to the neurosurgeon's office.

Dr. Grabb saw us promptly at our scheduled visit time. He was a neat man with a calming attitude. He began with the details of Kayla's diagnosis, the seriousness of her issues, his plan to do another MRI, and then surgery.

We asked a lot of questions about this new diagnosis, and he asked a lot of questions about Kayla's nerve disorder. I had always understood the brain to be the consistency of Jell-O, but Dr. Grabb explained in more detail. The brain enclosed *inside* the dura membrane is like Jell-O. The actual brain matter is like toothpaste, so in essence, Kayla's brain didn't have enough room, and it was being squeezed down into the top of the spinal cavity, trying to find more room.

When we ran out of questions, to my surprise he began to explain the surgery to us with Kayla in the room. At the time I understood that he thought surgery would be in the next few weeks, but we hadn't really had time to prepare our sweet almost-nine-year-old for what she was hearing. Several times her eyes grew large, but she just held my hand tighter.

The second MRI was scheduled, this time a C-spine, which would show images lower into the spinal cord. The biggest concern at this point was how many syrinxes were there. Was it just the one below the brain? Or could there be more?

The next day Kayla had her ninth birthday. We had a party scheduled for both the kids the following day, since their birthdays are three days apart, and so we made the cakes together on her birthday. She was very quiet, thoughtful, and helpful. I didn't know what was going through her mind, but I told her that if she wanted to talk about it, I was available for anything she wanted to discuss.

Kayla did ask a few questions that afternoon, but not many. She was handling all of it pretty well and with great calm. She looked up at one point and said, "I've been wondering how Jesus felt knowing that He had to go to the cross but didn't really want to. I have a feeling it was a little like what I feel right now. I know I need the surgery, but I don't want to have to go through with it." Her voice shook. "Is it okay to admit that I'm scared?"

I reached for my nine-year-old daughter and held her close. "Sure, baby, it's okay. Just remember that God is here. He's not going leave you. And when it comes time for the surgery, He'll be right there with you."

Kayla and I stood there, hugging and talking, covered in icing and flour, for almost 30 minutes. My whole body ached for the pain she carried inside her. Nine-year-old children are supposed to be thinking about a new bike, or dollhouses, or teddy bears. Not brain surgery.

The next few days passed by in a blur. Before we knew it Kayla had been through another MRI, and we were waiting in the neurosurgeon's office to hear his report. Dr. Grabb walked in and smiled. *I sure hope that means good news,* I thought.

Dr. Grabb explained that Kayla didn't have any more syrinxes on her spinal cord. He also said that he would like to wait a little while on the surgery. Kayla had been growing a lot, and they didn't want to do the surgery too soon and then have to go back in later because they hadn't created enough room. In other words, we would wait. And watch.

Our neurosurgeon explained what to be on the lookout for, and as I scribbled down notes, I had a feeling of dread in my stomach. How would I really know? What if I missed something vitally important? I reminded Dr. Grabb that Kayla didn't feel things like everyone else. He must have sensed my worry and told me that we would just need to keep a closer watch.

Kayla was ecstatic. Relieved that she didn't have to go through surgery just yet, she wanted to celebrate. I tried to catch her enthusiasm. I wanted to be happy about these new findings but something was holding me back. I prayed instantly for wisdom and guidance, as I didn't want to be a doubter.

The first few weeks passed in relative quiet. Kayla was happier, the kids were doing well in school, and I felt a smidgen of relief. But difficult decisions had to be made. We had a lot of medical bills, and they were just going to grow. The kids were finally covered with some insurance, but we were unsure as to how much it would pay toward the brain surgery.

We prayed about our decision and knew that we had to put the house up for sale. I called John, and he and his partner Jeff Morrell began the process.

As summer approached, two of our students from Alaska decided to come help us for their break. Lindsey Peterson and Joanna Beilfuss understood Kayla's disorder and had been with us through some of the hardest times. I desperately needed their help because during the summer, I couldn't get out with the kids unless I had an extra set of adult hands.

For instance, I couldn't drop Kayla at the door of a medical building all by herself to stand in the air-conditioning, and she couldn't go with me to park and then walk all the way into the building in 90-degree temperatures. And then there was grocery shopping: she couldn't be left by the freezer section while I loaded up the car and then drove it around the parking lot until the air was cooled off. Getting gas was just as much of an impossible situation. The car couldn't run while I filled up with gas, but then Kayla couldn't sit in the hot car. So someone would have to take her inside someplace that was cool enough.

Again, community and friends rallied around us. People donated items for garage sales to help with medical costs, groceries were donated, gifts were given.

One Saturday several wonderful women arranged a garage sale at my home. Lots of items were contributed, and it was one of the largest garage sales I'd ever seen. My friend Laura Howe was writing an in-depth article on Kayla, and she interviewed me while the ladies ran the sale. I was in the middle of a particularly emotional section when Chris brought a new neighbor over to the sale. Chris knocked on the door, and she introduced me to Lori Healy.

Lori was going through a really hard time. She was still settling into her new home, and her kids were far away for the summer. As we shared and cried together, I was blessed with another wonderful friend.

May was upon us, and Andrea Brown from the Colorado Springs *Gazette* did a front-page story on Kayla, titled "It's Not So Easy Being a Superhero."[1] The article was filled with warmth and grabbed your heart. Andrea did an amazing job.

We'd had dozens of newspaper articles written about our family before, but this one would change our lives.

An Incredible Visit

Jeff and John were trying to raise money for our family so that we could keep the house, but they were also beginning the process of marketing it. Lindsey and Joanna came for the summer and spent lots of time helping to finish the basement and painting it.

I was so thankful the girls came. It gave us a sense of normalcy, even though tension hovered as we kept a close eye on Kayla.

Things began to show up in Kayla that brought distress. She would stumble when she was walking, run into the doorjamb instead of walking through the entry, and one day at lunch, she was climbing onto a bar stool, missed it, and slammed her chin into the counter, spilling hot soup down the front of her. All of these things were logged into a notebook, and Dr. Margot, our pediatrician, became more and more concerned. Once again I was wearing down. I kept reminding myself to consider it joy. God knew what He was doing.

The worst part of all this was when Kayla started falling down the stairs. In the course of two months, she fell all the way down a flight of stairs seven times. Her frustration grew, even though she never said she was hurt. I would check her for bruises or broken bones and hold back my tears.

One afternoon we had all been painting down in the basement. Lindsey and Joanna told me they'd keep an eye on everything and clean up so I could take a shower. I ran up the two flights of stairs to our bedroom and was just about to hop in the shower when I heard a horrendously loud thumping sound. As I threw on my bathrobe, I heard Lindsey and Joanna yelling Kayla's name. Dread and fear took hold in the pit of my stomach.

The girls had told Kayla to change her shirt, since she'd accidentally run into a wall with wet paint on it. Kayla had changed and was going down the upper stairs when the girls were coming up the basement stairs, which were directly below. Somehow, Kayla lost her balance on the second to the top step and fell all the way down. The thumping that I'd heard was actually her little body hitting each step as she gained momentum and tried to stop her descent. Joanna and Lindsey in the staircase below her heard the deafening sounds that scared them beyond their imaginations. When we all reached her, Kayla was curled up into a little ball. She wasn't crying, and as I checked her body for broken bones, I began to worry at her lack of response. I pulled her onto my lap and told her she needed to talk to me.

"I'm fine," Kayla stated halfheartedly as she hugged my neck.

But I pulled back so I could look into her eyes and saw something else. She was frustrated.

Kayla slammed her hand on the step and said, "Why is this happening? I don't understand why I keep falling down."

We all sat at the bottom of the steps and prayed for Kayla. Joanna and Lindsey tried to cheer her up, but I couldn't bring myself to tell Kayla what we were all thinking. Even so, I think Kayla knew that these were all signs and symptoms, because she started feeling sharp pain in her stomach and was diagnosed with a stress ulcer soon after.

August arrived, and the heat was overbearing. The For Sale sign hung in the front yard, and I prayed every day that the Lord would send the right buyer for our home. One morning during my devotions, I picked up Kay Arthur's book *His Imprint, My Expression*. In the past I had loved going through this book, so I flipped the pages, looking for encouragement.

I stopped abruptly when I spied "When You Want to Call It Quits." I wasn't to the point of calling it quits yet, but I felt it coming. I needed to refuel; I needed to refresh my roots so I could stand up to the coming storms.

Kay's subtitle for that entry was "Are You Hanging on by Your Fingernails?" And that made me laugh—there were definitely days when I felt that way. But as I read her choice and encouraging words, I was convicted by them: "Tell God you want only what He wants—whatever that means."[2]

Ouch. I'd been praying for the Lord's will, but was I really okay with what His will entailed? *I* wanted my house to sell. *I* wanted to pay off all the bills. *I* wanted Kayla to get better and not have to undergo brain surgery. And not that those weren't good things, but were they what *He* wanted?

Kay ended that beautiful entry with Psalm 46:10–11, and as I held my Bible in my hands, my lips trembled as I read the words: " 'Be still, and know that I am God; I will be exalted among the nations, I will be exalted in the earth.' The LORD Almighty is with us; the God of Jacob is our fortress. Selah."

Lord, You are God, I prayed. *I know You have a plan. I will be still. I will rejoice. And I will wait on You. Your will be done.*

I woke up earlier than usual the next few days and spent more time in God's Word. I hadn't realized until that point how dry and shriveled my roots had become. I had been maintaining, not sustaining, and there was a huge difference.

One of those mornings I realized that I needed to write again. I'd made every excuse in the book for too long. My editor friend wrote me an e-mail later that day asking me if I'd worked on anything and encouraging me to please keep going. "Don't quit." Little did he know that his words would confirm what I felt I was supposed to do.

I joined American Christian Fiction Writers (ACFW) that very day. And in days I found myself surrounded with cyberfriends who all wrote. They encouraged me and prayed for me. It was an amazing step in my journey.

Several days later I was checking my junk e-mail folder when one particular e-mail caught my eye. The subject line read *Extreme Makeover: Home Edition*.

Huh. It's gotta be a scam. Just some sort of joke.

But something prodded me to open the e-mail. So I did.

The note was brief but explained that they had received a newspaper article about our family and were interested in hearing our story. I looked up at the clock and realized it was too late to call that day, but I asked Jeremy to come look at the e-mail.

Jeremy walked in, read the e-mail, shrugged his shoulders, and said, "Well, guess you better call them tomorrow." And he walked right back out. Yep, my Mr. Black and White. He kept me from dramatically going off the deep end on more than one occasion.

I stared at the screen a little while longer, and it dawned on me that my useless zoning out and rereading of a six-sentence e-mail really wasn't doing any good. Ever hopeful that I wouldn't stand in God's way, I turned off the computer and went to bed.

The next day we spoke with the show, and they told us they would like to send someone out to talk to us a little more.

The weekend they came to see us was a fun one. We hung out with them, we showed them around our house, and they looked at pictures and newspaper articles.

That night Kayla kept twitching her head in an odd manner. We were all exhausted and coming down from the exhilarating high of a day with "TV people," so I hadn't noticed anything up to that point.

Kayla moved her head back and forth, grabbing at the back of her neck with her hand. "Something's bothering me."

All my senses kicked into high gear. "What's bothering you, sweetie?"

"Something . . . back here." She continued to grab the back of her neck up near the base of the skull.

I scrambled into the kitchen to pick up the phone. I dialed Dr. Margot's number and explained what was happening. I could hear the edge of concern in her voice. But it was Saturday evening and going to the ER was never recommended for us. It took too long to explain the situation, and then there was the temperature issue. Dr. Margot asked me to watch her through the night and see if it was just the excitement of the day that was causing this symptom. We would touch base in the morning.

Kayla didn't sleep well that night. Whatever it was didn't register to her as pain, but it was a nuisance and kept her awake. Early the next morning Dr. Margot called. After filling her in on the details of the night, I knew this was it. There would be no more waiting. Brain surgery was imminent.

A Special Date

MRIs were scheduled, and after those we had appointments with the neurosurgeon. I'm so glad the Lord had given me the discernment that it was coming, because Dr. Grabb looked at me and informed me that we could no longer wait. I simply nodded in reply.

Dr. Grabb understood this would be hard for Kayla, so he asked her which date she would prefer. Kayla's favorite number is 26, so she picked the 26th of September. It wasn't even three weeks away.

We left the surgeon's office, but something caught Kayla's eye. I followed her gaze. There was a giant white tiger sitting on a top shelf. I smiled. She always was a stuffed-animal lover. As we climbed into the car, Kayla asked if we could look for a tiger.

I drove around town, calling everyone I could think of. There were so many things that needed to be taken care of, and not enough time to get it all done. My amazing friend, Joann, offered to make Kayla special nightgowns for the hospital and was crocheting a blanket for her. Jacque, Chris and Kelly Heitstuman, and my sister, Mary, were all on the look-out for giant stuffed tigers. And my friend Janelle, who worked on Kayla's feet, was checking into places that braided hair. Kayla didn't want to lose a lot of her hair, and I didn't want to brush her hair after the surgery and pull on her scar.

Two weeks before her surgery, Kayla was getting spoiled by Janelle with a manicure and pedicure. Janelle and I were discussing the vast improvement in Kayla's feet when the topic changed to the braiding of her hair. Every place that offered that type of braiding cost a lot of money, and money wasn't something we had an abundance of.

All of a sudden Janelle gasped and jumped up, grabbing her cell phone. "I have an idea!" And with that, she ran out the door.

Kayla had her feet soaking in the water and just looked at me and shrugged. In a matter of minutes, Janelle called me on my cell phone. Apparently she'd driven down the street to the Salon Professional Academy and told them about Kayla. She asked me if we could be there that afternoon.

Shocked, I told her yes, we could be there. Janelle then told me they were going to turn on the air-conditioning and be ready for us.

Several hours later we walked into the beautiful facilities of the Salon Professional Academy. I was pulling the portable ice chest, filled with extra packets, Josh had a book, and Kayla had her vest on. We were ready.

The young lady who was about to do Kayla's hair was not.

She looked a little shocked. We found out her name was Katelyn as I checked the temperature in the salon. Kayla sat in the chair, and Katelyn just looked at me.

"Why do you want to put cornrows in her hair?"

I tended to be a little matter-of-fact at this stressful point in my life. "Well, she has a really rare nerve disorder, and six months ago they discovered she has a rare brain malformation. She's having brain surgery in two weeks, and we'd like her to be able to keep as much of her hair as possible."

Katelyn's face began to pale.

"I figured if we got it out of the way, they wouldn't have to shave too much, and then we wouldn't have to worry about brushing it and tangles and all that jazz while she's healing."

Katelyn sat down. "Wow. That's really heavy."

I smiled at her. "We know that God's got a plan, and we're going to trust Him with the big stuff as well as the small stuff."

The beautiful young student seemed to be digesting all the information. She excused herself to get a drink of water and asked us if we needed anything. She came back with combs, clips, special little colored rubber bands, and a new determination. Her face glowed with a smile, and she looked ready to tackle Kayla's massive amount of long, thick blonde, hair.

Five and a half hours and 62 braids later, Katelyn had become part of the family. We talked about everything, and the kiddos adored her. She left us one more time and said she would be right back with someone special. It was then we were introduced to a neat lady named Kitty Victor. She was one of the owners of the Academy, and Katelyn had shared our story with her.

As Kitty and I talked, I felt an instant connection with that sweet woman.

We left the school with new friendships, encouragement, lots of prayer, and a whole lot of braids in Kayla's hair.

The Countdown

The week before surgery, Jeremy had some special things planned for us. We were given a special trip, so he sent the kiddos and me off to Denver to a fancy five-star hotel to spend a few days with our good friend Janelle Jay. Janelle had been in Louisiana with us when the kids were little but moved to Colorado soon after we moved to Alaska.

The hotel treated us with the greatest of care, and the kids enjoyed swimming in the pools. Janelle took us around to glow-in-the-dark miniature golf, ice-skating, and lots of good food. Josh and Kayla had never had the chance to ice-skate before, and so it was a fascinating new treat. I knew it would be a long time before Kayla would be allowed to do anything like it again, so I took lots of pictures, and we laughed at each other's antics.

While we were in Denver, Jeremy and several of my girlfriends packed up a lot of the house. I told him we would probably be taking a break from school to allow Kayla time to heal, so they packed up most of the schoolroom. Knickknacks, the china cabinet, and many other extra things were also on the pack list. Jeremy knew it would be a huge help to me to have a lot of the house packed, since it was still for sale and Kayla would be laid up for a little while.

Our fun time on our minivacation came to a close, and we loaded up and headed home. Kayla was doing remarkably well. We prayed a lot on the trip, Josh encouraged her, and we looked forward to getting the surgery over with.

I was amazed when we returned home and saw how much Jeremy and my friends had packed. The house looked great, and we were prepared for more showings. We needed the house to sell. We couldn't afford to keep it.

The last few days before her surgery, Kayla wanted to have swim lessons. Erica Duval rescheduled her life and met us at the pool several times during those days to work with her. I'll always appreciate the sacrifice of that wonderful lady. Kayla wanted to make sure she knew all the strokes and turns before she had to stop swimming for a while. So hours passed in the pool as she diligently worked with Erica.

September 25th was upon us, and my parents, Garry and Judy Hogan, arrived by plane. We met Erica at the pool for one last swim lesson before surgery, and Kayla enjoyed showing off her flip turn and strokes for her grandma and grandpa. Kayla wanted to eat out that night, so we all went out together. Kayla was chipper and enjoyed her special evening. My sister found a giant stuffed tiger and shipped it to us. Kayla planned on taking him and Big Bear to the hospital. She also had two smaller tigers that would make the trek with us.

We spent a lot of time in prayer that evening, and Kayla was able to go to sleep pretty quickly. I left her room and entered Josh's. He was beside himself with fear. My sweet 11-year-old with a huge heart ached for his sister. His mind was full of what-ifs and if-onlys. He wanted to help her but didn't know what to do.

I took Josh's hand, and we knelt by his bed. Tears choked us both, but we poured our hearts out to the Lord. All our fears, concerns, and thoughts. I was amazed at how much Josh truly understood about the seriousness of Kayla's surgery and how he was trying to be grown-up, but he still yearned to be a child and told that everything would be okay. I wrapped my arms around him, and he sobbed into my shoulder. I couldn't give sweet Josh any guarantees other than the fact that Kayla was in God's hands. And that was the best place she could be.

Josh was finally able to settle in for the night, and I left his room to go climb into bed. I was exhausted. My heart hurt. My shoulders hurt. And my eyes hurt. I reached our room and told Jeremy my woes. He held me as I cried softly, and we prayed together.

Consider it pure joy . . .

I know You've got this under control, Lord. I know You have Kayla in the palm of Your hand. I know she is Yours, Lord. But I would love to have her for longer . . . Please guide the surgeon's hand. Please heal Kayla.

Brain Surgery

We arrived at the hospital very early the next morning. Pre-op was completed, and Dr. Grabb came and spoke with us. Kayla's two small tigers were fitted with their own wristbands to take into the operating room (OR) with her, and they suited me up in scrubs so I could accompany her. Before I knew it, the time had come.

As they wheeled Kayla down the hall toward the OR, I prayed and attempted to keep my emotions in check. By the time we reached the OR, she was already almost out from the first medication. Thankfully they understood about Kayla's problems with sedation; using general anesthesia would be completely different. So with tears in my eyes, I told her I loved her and would see her when it was all over.

I was escorted out of the room, and the poor man who had that responsibility saw me lose it. I started sobbing and kept trying unsuccessfully to pull myself together. Thankfully there wasn't anyone else in the hallway to see me blubbering, because I definitely didn't want to upset anyone. But after holding everything in for so long, I couldn't stop the flow.

Several minutes later I sucked in a deep breath. I took off the scrubs, handed them to the man who patiently waited for me to get ahold of myself, and straightened my shoulders. I had to do this. *Lord, give me strength.*

I need more now than ever before. Help me through the next few hours. And please don't let me bite anyone's head off. Consider it pure joy, consider it pure joy, consider it pure joy . . .

I was shown the waiting area, where Jeremy, Josh, my parents, Chris, and Joann were all waiting. Sequestering myself in a corner, I sat and worked on a cross-stitch project Kayla had picked out. Josh and Jeremy worked on a massive LEGO project—a Star Wars Imperial Star Destroyer—and my friends chatted with my parents and others who were waiting.

I sat there working the needle and thread through the fabric and prayed. *Lord, I don't deserve Your grace. I'm so imperfect. I've made so many mistakes; I've sinned so much. Father, please forgive me. Kayla is Yours. She is in Your hands. I know You know my heart and what I want, but I do desire Your will for our lives. You've brought us through so many difficult circumstances, so many hardships, so many trials. I know You're here comforting and loving and taking care of us. Please help the surgeon, Lord. Please bring Kayla safely through this surgery, and please let it be successful . . .*

Peace flowed through me, and I held on for dear life. I had no desire to talk to anyone; I just wanted to get through the waiting time.

About an hour later the phone rang for the area we were in. A nurse told me that Kayla had made it through the preparation, and they were now beginning the surgery. She also said they would keep us informed as things progressed.

Another hour passed. When the phone rang again, I jumped for it. Kayla was doing well, and they were almost done.

Another phone call a little later told us that they were closing up.

Another hour passed, and Dr. Grabb came down the hall toward us. Jeremy and I went over to speak with him.

"Kayla is doing great. The surgery was very routine, almost boring if you want to put it in the sense that there were no surprises. But things were really, really tight in there."

I breathed in deeply as I let the first wave of relief wash over me.

Dr. Grabb continued, "We drilled out the bottom portion of the skull, the top two vertebrae, and opened the dura membrane and placed a dura graft in to give her brain more room. There was no need for any other procedures."

Jeremy and I nodded at the same time.

"She is in recovery and will be in PICU for a while. Mom, you can go up and see her soon, and then a family member or two at a time. As you know, the biggest risk of the surgery is opening the dura membrane. We will watch closely for infection, but we're expecting a full recovery. It will be very interesting to see if Kayla will be able to feel a little more after this."

We thanked the doctor, and Jeremy and I hugged. It was over. She was doing well.

A Sight for Sore Eyes

When they brought me up to see Kayla in the PICU for the first time, my heart did a flip-flop as I gazed down at my baby. Her face was severely swollen from being facedown on the operating table, and there were stitches behind both of her temples from where they'd bolted her head. But even with the blood and the stains on her gown, she was the most beautiful thing I'd ever seen.

A nurse was standing by a portable monitoring station, keeping track of all Kayla's statistics for the first few hours. She looked up at me and smiled as I walked to the side of Kayla's bed and kissed her forehead.

In the minutes that followed, I stood beside my daughter, holding her hand, and just enjoyed the sight of watching her breathe. Before too long

Kayla slowly opened her eyes and looked at me. That brief moment was so special. So much was communicated between the two of us without any words. With the slightest of smiles, Kayla went back to sleep.

I asked the nurse if it would be okay to bring up Jeremy and Josh now. She nodded, and I went back down to the waiting area to get them. I could tell that my sweet husband was chomping at the bit to see his little girl, and Josh was scared. When we stepped off the elevator, we walked down the corridor and through the secured doors for the intensive-care unit. I let Jeremy go in first, and I held Josh's hand as I tried to explain what he would see.

I've mentioned the bond between Josh and his sister before, but that day truly showed me how deep their relationship as siblings had become. My sensitive son walked forward to see Kayla, and his eyes grew larger and tearier with every step. He turned and buried his face in my shoulder. Kayla opened her eyes briefly again and saw Josh.

She spoke very softly in an attempt to comfort her brother. "I'm okay, Josh." And closed her eyes again.

Looking down at my son, I realized he was turning a pasty shade of white—and Josh has a dark complexion. I quickly told Jeremy that I thought Josh might be sick, so Jeremy rushed him out of the room and had our son put his head between his knees. He managed to get Josh into the elevator and back downstairs to my parents.

Back up in the ICU, Kayla woke up and asked if Josh was all right. The kid had just gone through brain surgery, and she was worried about her brother! That was precious to me. And even more so, my parents told me later how Josh continued to be concerned for his sister, and how much it upset him to see her lying in a hospital bed with machines all hooked up to her and blood on her head. The next day my parents took him to Build-A-Bear, where he made a special bear for Kayla and inserted a little voice chip that had a recording of Josh saying, "Hope you feel better, Kayla!"

Kayla was in PICU for two days. She was heavily medicated for a while but did really well when they took her off the meds. Maintenance had a fun time trying to keep our room cool enough, and the nurses had an interesting time every instance they asked Kayla, "How do you feel?"

The Lord did some amazing things in my heart that week. And I'm so thankful for the pruning and the growth. I kept reciting James 1:2–4 and Hebrews 12:1–3, knowing that He was using this time in my life for His purpose.

We have lots of stories from our time in the hospital, but one of my favorites is of a night in the PICU. Kayla woke up in the middle of the night and asked me to help her. I was immediately by the side of her bed, rubbing my eyes in an attempt to see straight. Kayla informed me that her legs were "diagonal," and I needed to fix them. *Oookaaayyy.* I didn't understand, but I straightened her legs.

Still half asleep I chuckled to myself. "Must be the medication."

A little later Kayla woke up suddenly again. "Mama! I need your help. My tongue is diagonal."

Oh, my. I laughed again. "Um, sweetie, I can't fix that for you. You have to fix that one yourself."

And on and on it went through the night. We still joke about Kayla's "diagonal" issues in the hospital.

By the end of the week, Kayla hadn't eaten much, but we had walked arm in arm for loop after loop around the nurses' station. Dr. Grabb came in to see her, and as Kayla begged him to go home, he told her he would agree on one condition: she had to eat.

We were going home! Jeremy, Josh, and my parents all came for the joyful celebration and loaded up all the stuffed animals and other gifts into the van. My parents had to fly back to Alabama, so they said their good-byes at the hospital, but we were so thankful they'd been able to come. Kayla had been so happy that they were there for her; Josh had some special time with Grandma and Grandpa, and they kept him occupied so he wouldn't worry too much about his sister.

Jeremy and Josh rode together while I drove Kayla in our van. I don't think we've driven so slowly, ever. The people passing us on the road surely must have thought we were insane, but I was so concerned about her hitting her head on the headrest that I really didn't care.

Kayla sighed when we pulled into our driveway. I could tell she was thrilled to be home. The guys unloaded the van as I slowly helped her walk into the house.

As soon as she was settled on the couch, the first words out of her mouth were, "I'm hungry. May I have something to eat?"

Sweeter words had never been spoken.

CHAPTER ELEVEN

That Famous Megaphone Announcement

The first few weeks of Kayla's recovery were slow. She had a hard time moving her head and rolling over, and sometimes she lost her balance when walking. Our first visit back with Dr. Grabb was eye-opening. The kind doctor was very honest with us about how "tight" things had really been inside her skull. MRIs hadn't shown what he found during surgery. His alleviated worry was clear on his face as he explained how thankful he was they had done the surgery when they had. The implications of his words didn't go unnoticed, and I thanked him profusely for all he had done for our little girl.

Chris, Kelly, and Jacque found two more giant tigers for Kayla. We now had a family of them occupying the living room, along with balloons, cards, and gifts.

Kayla was always very independent, but after the surgery she lost a little of that and wanted me right beside her. Her equilibrium was off, and she couldn't turn her head very well or change positions without assistance. So I found lots of things to do sitting next to her on the couch. We played games, made crafts, read books, and watched hours upon hours of *Little House on the Prairie*. We walked slowly around the house as she regained her balance and gradually maneuvered up and down the stairs. I would call Jeremy when it was time for lunch, so he could come home and sit beside her while I cooked.

With everything that happened, I had put my writing on the back burner again. But after all the hours sitting with Kayla, I started to realize that once more the Lord was placing the desire to write in my heart. I didn't have the time to get completely engrossed in the novel I was working on, because Kayla needed constant attention, and Josh needed special consideration through this difficult time as well. So I started to write more of my ideas down. Stories that had been brewing in my mind for a while, I finally put to paper. And as the creative process flowed out of me, I was impressed with the sensation of a great release.

I felt really bad for all the people who came to look at our house. They were all very interested, but we were unable to leave, and I think it was awkward for them, thinking they were invading. But we needed the house to sell, so the showings continued.

Kayla gradually livened up and lost the ever-present tired look. At the four-week mark, the doctor said it would be okay for her to get back in the pool. It would take a long time to fully recover and regain her stamina after neurosurgery. Each day Kayla spent a little more time in the pool, slowly working her muscles and building up her strength.

Kitty Victor from the Salon Professional Academy called me and asked if they could help. The school wanted to do a fund-raiser to help us with our giant medical bills. So one Saturday, hundreds of people from the community showed up at their doors and gave to our cause by having manicures and pedicures, and by having their hair cut, styled, and colored. More than 50 students donated their time and energy to help our family. It was one of the most incredible things I've ever seen and brought me to tears several times that day.

The media had really picked up on Kayla's story since the *Gazette* front-page article. Kayla was accustomed to the publicity, since it began before she could remember, but more and more people were calling wanting interviews. *The Montel Williams Show* called but didn't know that she had just undergone brain surgery. The producers talked to us off and on for a few weeks until we realized it just wasn't good timing for Kayla to travel.

It was amazing to me how many people commented, "Your story would be incredible for *Extreme Makeover*." And nobody knew they had contacted us. But as time moved on, I figured the show had chosen someone else. I was genuinely grateful that the producers had contacted us and visited, and if the only reason they came was for Kayla to show a symptom that put the wheels in motion for her surgery to take place, I would be eternally thankful.

Christmas came and went, and our house still hadn't sold. We couldn't afford the house payment *and* our bills, but we continued to survive each month. So many people jumped in and helped. Donations were sent to us, gift cards were mysteriously left on the front porch, and the organic-food stores had stepped in to offer assistance. We even received gift cards and checks for specific things. Some of the notes read, "Go buy some books for you and the kids," "Everyone needs shoes; get everybody a new pair of shoes," and even, "Go on a date with your husband," "Have lunch with a friend," "Go out and buy something fun." One day I even received a check with a note to go buy a video camera so we could film the kids. It was so amazing.

The housing market had plummeted, but we still had hundreds of showings. There were so many homes to choose from, I began to think most people wouldn't be able to remember which one was which.

One evening a family was coming to see the house. It was cool enough for us to go out, so we were preparing to leave when I heard Josh yell in panic. I was upstairs and scurried out of our room. Kayla was running up the stairs, her eyes huge, holding her left hand, both arms covered in blood.

"Mama, I'm hurt." No tears, no screaming, just a voice filled with fear as she watched blood seep from her thumb.

I took her to the bathroom and ran her hands under cold water so I could see the damage. Her left thumb was cut very deep directly across the knuckle. Kayla watched as blood seemed to pour from the wound and mix with the water swirling down the drain. She began to sway, and I looked at her face—she was white as a sheet.

Before I knew it, she passed out. I grabbed her as she fell, but her socks kept sliding on the floor. I couldn't keep her thumb over the sink and hold her upright for very long. I quickly scanned the bathroom, trying to find a way to lay her down and not hit the scar in the back of her head. All I could think about was the fact that just a few months before, she'd had brain surgery. *Lord, help me get her safely down.*

I finally maneuvered my tall girl, slippery socks and all, onto the floor with a towel underneath her head. I held her arm up in the air, hoping I could stop the bleeding and get her thumb bandaged. The slice in her thumb needed stitches, but when I called Dr. Margot, she recommended a liquid bandage since it was so late in the day, and this was Kayla. We couldn't just head to any old medical office where it would be too hot.

Once Kayla revived, I learned that she had gotten impatient with Josh as he tried to open something. Josh is extremely careful and cautious (and thus slow) because he does feel pain. And Kayla isn't supposed to use scissors or knives of any sort unless an adult is present. But both the children knew we were in a hurry to leave before the people arrived for the showing. So, using my kitchen shears, she didn't realize her thumb was in the way until it was too late.

It was a crazy evening, but Kayla looked up at me from the floor and told me she was sorry for getting impatient with Josh and disobeying. Her beautiful blue eyes expressed her remorse. It was a hard lesson to learn, but she understood in a whole new way why she needed to be more cautious. Watching her own blood flow down the sink scared her.

We received an offer on the house after that showing in late February. It was exciting and depressing all at the same time. We were so thankful the house finally sold but sad to see it go. The contracts were signed, but we had a new obstacle to overcome: Where would we move?

Our budget was very small, so to find homes in our price range, we had to look *way* out of town. We even had friends who owned land who were willing to work with us, as well as a manufactured-home place that worked with us, but it was still going to cost too much money. We needed space, since we were home all the time, but we also needed an environment that was clean and had air-conditioning. Unfortunately we couldn't find any of those things. So Jeremy started searching for foreclosed homes. This became yet another adventure for me, as well as another lesson on pride.

John Unzueta took us to every one of the homes Jeremy found. He spent day after day looking with us. Several times we'd find one we were excited about only to find out that an offer had already been made that day. The good ones went really fast. The others . . . well, let's just say I literally ran out of several of them.

My most memorable foreclosed-home visit happened early one afternoon. John had just come from showing a house worth well over a million dollars. He was dressed very nicely. I had just come from a ladies' get-together and was dressed very nicely. Jeremy had just come from the church—and you guessed it—he was dressed very nicely.

Knowing how "icky" some of these homes could be, I left Josh and Kayla in the car. The guys and I went in.

It wasn't pretty.

All the light fixtures had been yanked out of the ceiling. The appliances were all gone, and there were holes in the walls. And to make my OCD tendencies shoot through the roof, there were so many "droppings" on the floor that I hesitated before I took each step.

John had a great sense of humor as he and Jeremy tried to help me see the potential of the house. They were talking new paint and carpet. I was thinking 500 gallons of bleach.

The moment of my complete undoing came when John walked out of the bathroom. He held up his hand and said, "I'm sorry, he didn't make it."

"What?" Fear only began to describe my thoughts at that moment. "Who didn't make it?"

John laughed at me as I approached him, but he held up his hand again to stop me. "It's just a mouse. He's dead. In the toilet."

"Ewwww!!" I did that little girly dance that most of us of the female gender do when a mouse is even mentioned. "Can't you flush it?"

"Um, no." John continued to laugh at me. "It's frozen in a block of ice."

I tried to keep an open mind, since Jeremy seemed to be really interested in the house. But I was definitely the first one out of the house as soon as he gave the signal. John pulled antibacterial wipes out of his car, and I pulled out baby wipes. I never touched anything in that house, but still I scrubbed my hands. And the bottom of my shoes.

Our house hunt continued until we finally found a foreclosure that was livable, had air-conditioning, and was the right price. It wasn't anything grand, but we were happy nonetheless.

The week of the kiddos' birthdays arrived in March. We were supposed to close on our new house on Monday, and the old house on Friday.

Monday morning, we were at the pool, and I was looking forward to signing the papers that afternoon when I received a call from the mortgage company for the new house. They had worked with us and knew our situation—and the individual attention to our needs had been wonderful. But the news they had to share that morning was not so wonderful. The mortgage market had bombed. Underwriters were knee jerking, and all of a sudden they wanted $20,000 up front to seal the deal. We didn't have $20,000. The mortgage company knew this, but they had to pass along the devastating information. Not only could the house not be ours, but we couldn't qualify for *any* house anymore.

A Minor Setback and a Miracle

I called Jeremy and tried not to cry. It was actually Kayla's birthday, and I was determined not to let this little "house thing" get me down. We knew we needed a plan—we had people buying our house on Friday. Jeremy told me he would start making phone calls and see what he could find out about rentals. I would call John and enlist his help once again, and after we left the pool, the kids and I would drive around looking for For Rent signs.

The day passed in a crazy blur of house hunting. Kayla and Josh were great sports, often sitting in the air-conditioned car, never complaining as Jeremy and I traipsed in and out of the houses. If one was cool enough, they could look inside too.

One of the first houses we saw had my favorite floor plan from Premier Homes. It was the house we would have built had we had the money, but I didn't think we would be able to afford the rent. I called and left a message, but it wasn't until later in the day that the property manager had time to call me back. We scheduled a time for the following evening, and I continued to drive around looking for other homes to rent.

The next day Kayla had her six-month MRI and follow-up with Dr. Grabb. Jacque, Garrett, and Brandi came with us. We went straight from the imaging center to the surgeon's office, and the doctor smiled brightly as we entered.

"It's gone," he said and motioned for me to follow him. As we entered another room, I immediately saw the screens with several of Kayla's MRIs pictured on them. I gasped when I saw the last one. I knew what he meant.

"It's completely gone," Dr. Grabb repeated. "I've never seen anything like it. You can't even see where it was."

"God is so cool," I whispered.

The doctor pointed to another area on one of the screens. "See here? The brain has moved all the way back up to where it should be. And the syrinx is . . . gone."

I stuck in again, "God is cool."

"I've never seen a more perfect post-op MRI." Dr. Grabb grinned from ear to ear.

Our neurosurgeon went on to explain in medical terms all the intricacies of what was on those screens. But for me, I saw with my own eyes in the images on the screen the fact there was no longer a "hole" in her spinal cord. Nothing was better than those moments of praising God for what He'd done in Kayla.

Dr. Grabb looked at Kayla and told her to go ride her bike and be a kid. He even said that he didn't need to see her for another year unless there were problems. That fact was extraordinary.

Kayla began to jump up and down and ran out of the room, yelling as she went, "It's gone!"

The kids all jumped around with Kayla while Jacque and I cried. It was hard to believe. All the doctors had tried to prepare us for the possibility that the syrinx would be permanent, or at the very least would take years to go away. It had been a mere six months. What a miracle!

Our focus quickly turned back to the task at hand; we still had to find a place to live. Our search that day brought several possibilities, but when we visited the home built by Premier, I knew it was the one we wanted.

The property manager and owners worked with us on the rent and were very generous with their time. The owners installed air-conditioning into their brand-new home, and we were allowed to move in ASAP. Jeremy sold his car, and we were loaned money to make the deposit and first month's rent. It would all be over soon—the house would be sold, and we would try to get back on our feet and pay off all the bills.

Two days later we moved into the rental house.

Mrs. Paul and a Dragon Conversation

Life had been hard for my Josh, as can be imagined. I was always searching for something special—something just for him. The amazing author Donita K. Paul was in my local writer's group, but I didn't know her very well. One day I noticed her DragonKeeper series of books in the store and picked them up for Josh.

He devoured them.

So the next time she had a book signing close to us, I asked Jeremy to stay home with Kayla so I could take Josh to meet Donita.

Josh is a very creative guy. Always has been. After reading Donita's books, his imagination took off with the world she had created. He even had his own dragons, with names, colors, and talents.

As we stood in line to see her, she noticed me and waved. *What a neat lady*, I thought.

We reached the front of the line, and she pulled Josh behind the table to talk to her. Her publicist and marketing people came out to talk with me while she focused her complete attention on my son. Her face lit up with excitement in their special conversation, and I kept stealing glances in their direction. I wanted to cry, laugh, and sing all at the same time. Donita gave Josh exactly what he needed. Wings to soar.

After their chat she waved me over, and I hugged her neck.

As I drove home that afternoon, I asked Josh about his adventure at the book signing. He raved about the new book, how he couldn't wait to read it, and how Mrs. Donita had talked to him in "dragon language." I wasn't exactly sure what that meant, but to Josh it meant the world.

Over the next few weeks and months, Donita called us and visited our home. She asked Josh to help her come up with new dragon names, and she became my mentor and dear friend. Kayla loved her so much that she decided she'd better read those "really cool" books Josh kept talking about.

In every situation God has given us a community of friends and loved ones who reach out, love us, and lift us up. In the case of Donita K. Paul, I felt like Anne Shirley in *Anne of Green Gables*. I had been given a kindred spirit.

How Many Times Can One House Sell?

Friday arrived, and I found out the closing on our house had been postponed. After the nightmare we'd just gone through with our own mortgage woes, we figured the buyers' mortgage company was probably asking for more money or paperwork as well. We waited through the weekend and several days into the next week until Jeff called with news.

The deal fell through.

Uh-oh. We now had a rental house, which was the roof over our heads, and the house that we owned, which we couldn't afford.

I called our mortgage company, hoping that someone would listen to our story and help.

Ever the optimist and people truster, I wasn't prepared for the not-so-helpful response. Basically, I was told that they didn't care. They couldn't help. They wouldn't help. The market was a mess, and they all had piles upon piles of foreclosure paperwork on their desks. The only way it would matter to them was if we got "severely" behind in our payments.

I hung up the phone feeling as if I had been run over by a truck. We weren't behind yet, but it didn't take a genius to figure out we couldn't pay a mortgage *and* rent, so it wouldn't be long before we met their criteria.

Once again I stopped writing. Oh, my excuses were good: not enough time, with trying to sell the house and homeschooling, and the children needed me. My wonderful writer friends kept encouraging me, trying to prod me along, but I allowed myself to wallow in self-doubt. Life was just too hard right then.

More and more people looked at our house, but it still didn't sell.

The month of May came, and with it came another one of our former students from Alaska, Holly Volstad. She was going to stay with us for the summer to help, and she got a job with the YMCA. Holly brought even more liveliness to our household. Her tradition had been to come only for Thanksgiving, since it was too costly to fly all the way home to Alaska from college. She decided to stay, and we found out what a joy it was to have her around permanently. Kayla and Josh had a special attachment to Holly, which went all the way back to Kayla's really sick days in Alaska.

The brightest spot of that summer was the introduction of a new neurologist for Kayla—Dr. Stephen Smith.

Now, Dr. Smith had his work cut out for him. Kayla wasn't too fond of doctors after all she'd been through, including brain surgery. So when we arrived at our appointment, I prayed for her to at least talk to him. I couldn't blame her for not wanting to be social; after all, the kid had gone through hundreds, if not thousands, of doctors' visits over the years. But my heart yearned for her to have an extraordinary connection so that she would trust her specialist.

My prayers would be answered that day.

Dr. Smith talked to us for a long time. He was patient and kind, with a very homey atmosphere around him. His office didn't scream of hospital visits, sterile equipment, and needles. He left the room for a few minutes to take an urgent call, and as soon as he walked out the door, Kayla said, "I like him a lot, Mama."

I was speechless at that point. The only other doctors she had said that about were Dr. Margot, our current pediatrician, and Dr. Baker, our pediatrician in Alaska. She had eventually warmed up to other doctors, but to state that she liked him on the very first visit was indeed that extraordinary connection I was looking for.

Dr. Smith came back in the room a few minutes later, and we finished our appointment. A little while later we exited the room, and Kayla headed off to the bathroom. I pulled Dr. Smith aside and told him about Kayla's little revelation. He responded with such a genuine smile, it warmed my heart.

And then the real shocker came.

Kayla skipped out of the bathroom—right up to Dr. Smith—wrapped her arms around him, and hugged him.

Dr. Smith hugged her right back and told her that he was honored to have her as a patient.

Ever since that day Kayla can't wait to go to the neurologist. Even if something is wrong, she loves to see him, trusts him, and knows that he will take good care of her.

Kayla's eczema flared up severely on her legs that summer. I thought it had begun to heal when one night she scratched until it looked as if she'd been clawed by a wild animal. The next morning I went to help her cream her legs and was shocked at the sight. I called Dr. Margot's office, and they told us to come in immediately.

The news would not be good. Kayla had opened up some serious wounds and had a double infection. It appeared that she had scratched and then rubbed her calves together in her sleep, trying to alleviate the itch. This only spread the infection into all the areas she had scratched open. Dr. Margot wanted to admit her to the hospital but knew that was quite a feat without advance notice for the temperature. There'd been too many close calls lately with her overheating, and Dr. Margot didn't want to take the risk.

Instead, Kayla had two massive—and I do mean *massive*—shots in her arms, some serious antibiotics, and lots of special creams. Our incredible pediatrician was seriously worried about the infections entering the bloodstream, which could be deadly.

As Kayla healed from the intense infections, June rolled around, and we received another offer on the house.

A couple of weeks later, it fell through.

July approached, and another offer came in.

This time our mortgage company went in—they winterized the house and put a steel plate over the door—because we *were* now behind on our payments, and they knew we weren't living in the house.

Our Realtors frantically tried to get the keys, because we had an offer on the house. But by the time the mortgage company got around to giving the keys to them, yet another buyer had walked.

By this point I was just ready for the house to foreclose. I had no idea what that process entailed, but it had to be better than all the phone calls I was receiving, telling me I was the scum of the earth because I hadn't paid my mortgage. When the phone calls started, I had patiently tried to explain our situation and asked if they would help. After 50 or so calls, I was humiliated and beginning to believe I truly *was* the scum of the earth. They wanted their money, which was rightfully theirs, and I couldn't give it to them.

My humiliation seemed complete when the mortgage company sent me a newspaper article in the mail, with my name in bold lettering, announcing the public auction of my home. Set for my birthday, no less.

Consider it pure joy, consider it pure joy, consider it pure joy . . .

Life is hard, but God is good.

I pasted on a smile and knew we would be okay. God was in control. Even if that meant losing everything. It was all just stuff, anyway. Right?

Jeff called the next day with good news. We had another offer. I tried to get excited, but with the track record we were having, I was unsure. Jeff offered to pay for all the utilities to come back on so that the inspection could take place. Things were moving along.

The goal was to get the house sold before the public auction could take place. I didn't understand all the legalities, but I knew that certain things had to be filed by a certain time.

The day of the inspection went beautifully. Absolutely nothing had to be fixed. The buyers were happy, we were happy; it all seemed to be working out.

But the following day the buyers went back with their agent to measure something or look at something. I just know they were looking at the house that they were excited about buying.

Their agent called Jeff to inform him that the basement was flooded. Yep, you read that right. Flooded.

When Jeff called me, he told me I wasn't going to believe it. And he was right. But apparently whoever had winterized the basement for the mortgage company had left the valve open on the hot-water heater. When the water was turned back on, the hot-water heater filled up, overflowed, and filled up the basement. Fortunately we had a sump pump down there, but my sweet husband had finished that basement himself. All his hard work flooded.

I started laughing. I told Jeff I felt sorry for him—and I felt bad that we were the "thorn in his side."

Considering this new trial as joy came a little easier. There'd been so many disappointments and letdowns and hard times that it became a habit to hear the words in my head, "Don't quit. Keep going." I called our homeowner's insurance company and tackled the problem at hand. There were still buyers for the house, but there was a flooded basement.

The beginning of August was hot. Jeff had gone through all the legal channels to get the public auction on the house delayed so that we had a little more time to sell our house. Our insurance was handling the basement issue, and we prayed daily not to have another setback.

Jeremy was getting a little discouraged. He was working his rear end off and just wanted to provide for us. But the cost of living in Colorado and the massive amounts of medical bills were pulling us down. We lay in bed one night, hashing out our options. Again I had that overwhelming peace and joy flow through me, and I knew all the material junk was just that: material junk. I understood how discouraging it was for Jeremy, but I told him we could live in an air-conditioned box, and as long as we were together, nothing else mattered.

My husband smiled and held me close. We spent a good portion of the night praying and giving our needs over to the Lord.

There were going to be trials.

There were going to be really tough times.

There were going to be days we wanted to call it quits.

But we would keep going—and consider it joy.

An Extraordinary Introduction

My birthday is in August, and my friends Mary, B.J., Jacque, Holly, and I were all going to a David Phelps concert. David was my favorite musician, but I'd never had the chance to see him in person. The day of the concert, Jacque called and said that she and her kids had pinkeye, so she couldn't go.

Kayla overheard the conversation, and as soon as I shut my phone, she asked, "Mama, if we bring all my cooling gear and the fans, and I wear my vest and my hat, can I please, please go?"

My heart ached for Kayla because I knew she loved David Phelps, but I had to tell her she couldn't come with me. I knew there was no way the church would be cool enough, especially with a large crowd and all the body heat.

My sweet girl didn't whine or complain. She understood, but it was still hard for my 10-year-old, whose favorite song was "End of the Beginning." I offered the ticket to my friend Joann, and she said she would love to go.

A little later, Kayla tapped me on the shoulder. "May I use my allowance money to buy a CD from Mr. David? I'd like to have one of my own."

She never ceased to amaze or impress me. Kayla was so sincere, was so gracious, and always rolled with the punches. I told her that I would buy her one of her very own, and I would ask Mr. David if he would sign something for her as well.

Jeremy made sure he could stay home with the children so that I could have this special night out. Holly and I left superearly for the concert. We were excited and wanted to be the first ones in the door. We arrived so early that the church personnel invited us in to visit with them. The doors opened, and we found our seats. Mary, B.J., and Joann met up with us soon after, and the concert began.

It was an amazing night, filled with incredible music and the abundantly talented Mr. Phelps. As the evening drew to a close, I couldn't stop smiling. I had been refreshed.

Mary and B.J. needed to get back home, so Joann, Holly, and I stood in line to see David. I had brought special paper and a pen to ask him to sign for Kayla, and I purchased something for her and for Josh.

We tried to stay at the back of the line so I wouldn't waste everyone else's time while I explained Kayla's story. I thought about what I would say and kept coming up blank. Hopefully I could at least get the point across that he had an amazing little 10-year-old fan.

By the time we reached David, it was late. We were all tired, and I felt bad for wanting a little more of his time.

I walked up to him and said, "My daughter . . . ," but nothing else would come out. I sobbed. And I mean *sobbed*. Here I was, in front of David Phelps, crying my eyes out, and the poor man had no idea why. It wouldn't have surprised me if he had called for someone to escort the "hysterical woman" out the door.

But being the gentleman he is, David just reached out and said, "Are you okay?"

Thankfully Holly and Joann knew our story backwards and forwards. As they spilled their hearts out to David, he listened intently, and I tried to pull myself together.

I think David was overwhelmed by the seriousness of our story—it is pretty intense, especially when it's given to you all at once in a 60-second blurb—but he graciously took the paper for Kayla and wrote her a special note.

I had just stopped crying when I watched him carefully choose his words and write an entire page. The tears flowed again. I was hoping for "To Kayla, Love, David Phelps." And yet he poured out so much more. He was sharing a piece of his heart with my little girl.

David asked for our contact information, and he took a picture with us. When Holly and I reached the van, I asked her to run back inside to thank him. I wanted to make sure he understood how truly grateful I was.

I drove home bubbling over with excitement to give the kiddos their gifts. It had been an amazing night, and David made a huge impression with his sincerity and care.

Little did I know that Kayla had made a huge impression on him as well.

When Kayla's temperature issues worsened, we had to stay home from church. After overheating one Sunday morning, I knew it was just too much for her system to handle. So the kids and I started having our own church service. A couple of weeks after David's concert, Josh, Kayla, and I were snuggled on the couch doing our Bible study. As we were praying, my cell phone rang. I looked at the caller ID but didn't recognize the number.

"Hello?"

"Kim?"

I tried to place the voice but couldn't quite recognize it with the one word. "Yes, this is Kim."

"Hi! This is David Phelps."

Well, of course it was. I mean, really, the amazingly talented, super-famous David Phelps calls all the time, right?

Needless to say I was shocked. "Well, hi!"

After talking to me for several moments, David asked to speak with Kayla, and a better gift he couldn't have given her. Their conversation was so stinking cute from what I heard. Kayla smiled from ear to ear and kept saying, "Yes sir, uh-huh, yes sir, uh-huh, yes sir, uh-huh." My heart soared with gratefulness for this big-hearted man who took the time to talk to a very special little girl, who was now officially his biggest fan.

Public Auction Number Two

All the house junk at this point had gotten ridiculous. It seemed every day that something else needed to be done, another paper needed to be signed. And then, after all the paperwork, all the driving to the courthouse, all the chaos, they still announced that our house would go back up for public auction in September.

The buyers wanted the house, and we wanted to sell it to them. But the mortgage companies were taking their sweet ole time. Now we had another deadline—and I was afraid we wouldn't make it. The ramifications of foreclosure still hung over my head, but there were days I just wanted it to be over. Jeff and John were working on our crisis constantly, but they were wearing thin as well. Our situation was a tough one, and I'm so thankful they stuck by us through it all.

The day for the public auction was only a week away. Jeff scrambled with the mortgage company and lawyers to try to postpone it even by a day.

Labor Day came and went.

We still didn't close.

Jeff was able to postpone the auction for one week, and then it would all be over if we couldn't close in time.

I kept my chin up. I held on to my joy. But there were days I felt like a horrible person because I couldn't afford to keep my house. I knew we had done the right thing. Our priorities were straight, but not everyone knew the details and the story. Once again I worried about what people thought.

Two days later the call finally came. We would close the next day.

As we gathered in the title-company's office, Jeff and I joked about how far we'd come. It had *only* taken a year and half for our beautiful house to sell. It would probably go down in his history book of "hardest sales." The papers finally arrived, and we sat down to sign.

It was over.

Finally.

We had lost everything we put into that house—all the savings, all the finishing of the basement, all the equity—but it was over. The house had sold.

One-Year Celebration

The one-year anniversary of Kayla's brain surgery arrived on September 26, 2007. We bought pink balloons, pink streamers, and paper plates. I made a cake, and we had a party.

As I watched Kayla play with her friends, I thought about how amazing our great God truly is. If you were to look at her, you'd never know she'd gone through brain surgery—or that she suffered from an extremely rare nerve disorder.

The day was a joyous one. Jeremy and I promised each other we wouldn't talk about bills or finances or "what now?" We'd just enjoy the precious time together and be thankful for Kayla's incredible recovery.

A special e-mail arrived from David Phelps, expressing his celebration with us at the momentous landmark. Kayla smiled from ear to ear. I was amazed again at the outpouring of love for our precious daughter and our family.

The kids and I prayed every day about our opportunity with *Extreme Makeover*. We understood we were finalists, but that meant there were other families who needed a home just as much as we did, if not more. We didn't know who they were, but we prayed for those families as well, and for all the other people who struggled. The rental house was amazing; we loved it and were so thankful for a roof over our heads, but it wouldn't be ours forever. The owners had bought it as their retirement home, and eventually they would want to move in.

Josh and Kayla had great attitudes about the whole situation. I told them that as long as we were together as a family, everything else didn't really matter.

A Bus, a Design Team, and the Surprise of Our Lives

Sunday, September 30, 2007, is a day none of us will easily forget. It was midmorning when we heard Ty Pennington, of *Extreme Makeover: Home Edition*, shout through his megaphone, "Good morning, Woodhouse family!"

I remember our collective intake of breath, as if there wasn't enough air in the room to fill our lungs. My feet stuck to the floor as the reality poured over me, so Jeremy gently nudged me from behind and said, "Run!"

Kayla's and Josh's faces were all smiles as they made a mad dash out the front door into the Design Team's arms.

I cried. A lot.

I couldn't believe they had actually shown up. Things like this didn't happen to real people—or so I thought. Were they actually going to build us a house in seven days?

Yep.

And it was going to be safe and healthy for Kayla and Josh?

Yep.

And . . .

Our lives would never be the same.

CHAPTER TWELVE

That's What Love Is

The *Extreme Makeover* team was amazing.

Genuine. Energetic. Loving. These are just a few words that describe all the wonderful people. Ty is an incredible person who throws his heart and soul into each family. I know he's followed by thousands of fans everywhere and probably doesn't get much time for himself; yet he came into our home and treated us with great care and respect. The privilege of speaking with him one-on-one was like talking to a longtime friend. His emotion and depth are real, and his special concern for kids shines through in what he does.

Ed was hilarious. And one of the sweetest people I've ever met. When he came through the door to talk with us, I was amazed at how tall he was. I asked him about the hand he injured carving an American flag for another EMHE family, and he showed me his scar. But what impressed me most were his questions that first day. He sincerely tried to wrap his mind around all the details of Kayla's condition. He wasn't being filmed. He was simply interested and concerned about the details. As a mom, that impressed me beyond anything I could have imagined.

Then there was Matt, our builder. He came to meet us briefly before we were whisked away for our extreme vacation. He walked straight up to Jeremy and me and hugged our necks. He had given himself a crash course on our story that day so that he could truly understand our needs. As we spent a few minutes talking, I was in awe of his knowledge and under-standing. And then he asked Jeremy a question: "If there's one thing you need with the home to ensure the safety of your family, what would it be?"

Jeremy looked emotional as he pondered the question. "Matt, I can imagine you probably know that climate control is our biggest need. But I have to say thank you so much for asking. Because for me, as a dad who has to leave them and go to work, it would mean so much to know that there is a backup in case the power goes out."

Matt gripped Jeremy's shoulder and squeezed it. "I understand that completely. Let me see what I can do."

In a whirl of amazing events, our week with *Extreme Makeover: Home Edition* began.

The Build

The seven days of our Extreme Makeover were intense, exhilarating, ex-citing, and filled with surprise after surprise. The first of which was the location of our vacation. We were going to Breckenridge, Colorado—chosen for its low average temperature. The Extreme Team had done their homework, knew our story well, and prepared the best possible time for our family.

Breckenridge is a beautiful community. We had a great drive up and looked forward to the temps being just right for Kayla to be able to par-ticipate in outdoor activities.

Carly Grimes, from the Breckenridge resort chamber, called and told us that if we needed anything at all, she was available. Full of a wealth of knowledge about the area, Carly was able to arrange some amazing activ-ities for us that suited our needs. The kids adored her. We had a blast in the quaint mountain town—ice-skating, visiting a gold mine, rock climbing, and just walking outside. The Extreme Team's choice had been great.

We received quite a few odd looks as we requested to sit outside and eat in the 50-degree temperatures, but it was so much fun. For a family that doesn't get the opportunity to eat out much, it was indeed a two-for-one treat—a chance to be outside *and* a chance to dine away from home. While the rest of the patrons chose their warm and cozy environment inside, with fireplaces ablaze, we chose the cool weather, seemingly special ordered just for us, the wind on our faces, and the panoramic and majestic mountain views.

Many people have asked me what that week was like. Did I imagine what the house would be like? Did they really build it in seven days? Was it really a surprise?

The entire experience was more than amazing. More than incredible. More than mind-boggling. Each time I thought about where we were, why we were there, and what was happening, my mind went blank. How could I possibly imagine the events taking place back in the Springs? I couldn't even believe I was in Breckenridge! It all seemed like a dream. Watching Kayla walk among the trees laden with crimson and golden leaves warmed my heart. She was outside, having the time of her life. Josh and Kayla swam in a pool that was indoors *and* outdoors, they panned for gold, and the scoreboard at the Breckenridge Ice Arena scrolled all week with "Welcome Woodhouse Family." It was indeed a surreal time.

But something I will forever remember is the expressions on my children's faces. All the emotions and feelings encompassed in that week were so preciously displayed—excitement, happiness, faith, joy, relief. They had no problem believing that we'd been given that incredible opportunity. I laughed as I admonished myself in my thoughts: *Oh, Kim—oh, ye of little faith.*

During the week, Ty and the Extreme Makeover crew kept us up to date via video with the happenings back in the Springs. We were given the opportunity to watch the bulldozers and workers as they came parading in, and Ty's humorous demolition of a miniature model house.

As I watched the screen, I realized there were hundreds, if not thousands, of people, all sacrificing and working on our behalf. I knew at that moment what community was all about. There was a need, and people poured out themselves to meet that need.

From the beautiful young ladies who sang the National Anthem to all the workers clothed in their blue Extreme Makeover shirts and hard hats, the smiles and tears stretched across the community and will forever be burned into my memory.

Another incredible occasion of the week was meeting Gabby Gingras in person.

Until Kayla was seven years old, we knew of no other child or person in the world with the same disorder. And then we heard about Gabby. A friend had seen her on the local news in Minnesota, and I called the news station to ask them to pass our information on to Gabby's family. We were so excited to touch base with another family dealing with a lot of the same issues, and we hoped we could help one another through the tough times. As time passed, our relationship grew. Gabby's mom was the one who brought us together with Dr. Smith. Kayla loves Dr. Smith. But the neatest part of the story is that he's Gabby's neurologist as well, and to know that he works with another patient who has HSAN is a huge relief for us.

The Gingras family started a foundation to help other kids with this really rare disorder, and over the years the foundation, Gift of Pain, helped us in a huge way as well. But even with all the contact, e-mails, and phone calls, we'd never had the chance to meet, until Ty brought Gabby to see Kayla.

The time with Gabby and her mom was precious. Kayla loved meeting someone with her same diagnosis for the very first time. And as moms, Tricia Gingras and I cried, hugged, and laughed together over the wonderful meeting.

Later in the week another huge surprise was given to our family. We watched via video as David Phelps came to Colorado Springs to do a special benefit for our family. As he sang "That's What Love Is," tears sprang to my eyes, and the words washed over me. My respect and admiration grew for the incredible musician.

The words to his song branded my heart. That's what the whole build was about. It's why the community came together.

Love.

Helping someone in need. Giving of yourself to raise someone else up.

The lines in the bridge are what got to me the most. "It's reaching out and holding on so someone else will know. Love is in the not letting go."

My hope had been that other people would see that in *our* lives. We weren't perfect. But we were holding on and not letting go.

David spoke into the camera just for us that night. It was a special message, conveying the depth of his heart—and his love for people. That's what love is.

Reveal Day

The week flew by, and before we knew it, we were on our way back to Colorado Springs, in a limo, about to see our new home. This was the part that scared me most. Oh, not the house—I knew we would be completely happy and thankful for whatever they built—but the whole "move that bus" moment had my mind spinning in circles. I worried as the week went on. It had been really hot when we left. What was the weather like now? What if it was too hot? Kayla wouldn't be able to stand out in the sun to film the part everyone looks forward to in the show. I was assured that they had a backup plan and not to worry. They truly did think of everything and had taken care of all of our needs, but as a mom, I was the one used to controlling Kayla's environment and making sure she was safe. And I had no idea how they were going to pull it off.

But again, I shouldn't have worried. God is in control. And it was apparent to everyone I talked to that day that Someone was looking out for Kayla. You see, the entire week of the build had been really hot.

Reveal Day was cold. And I mean *cold*.

Kayla didn't even need to wear her vest outside. It was incredible.

The weather the next day?

Hot. And on the front page of the *Gazette* was a story titled "One Cool Makeover."[1]

A Fresh Start

Matt Swanson of Premier Homes was our builder. And let me tell you that man has a heart of gold. We'd met oh so briefly that first day, but it all rushed by in a blur, and I had a hard time believing he was real. His beautiful wife, Shannon, is another angel in my life. She spent countless hours on the phone and in the planning, never taking credit for anything—never wanting attention on herself. Only because of my persistent questioning did I find out the lengths she had gone to in helping the build happen. Matt's parents, Bev and Duayne, were a huge part of the experience as well. The beautiful ironwork in our home was handmade by Duayne. Every time I touch or see his exquisite craftsmanship, I smile. I wonder if any of them slept during the whole build.

When we moved into our new home that week, Matt was like a little kid, showing us all the amazing and special little things that we hadn't had time to see or hear about before. If you watched the show, when the bus moved, my husband said, "That's the house we wanted! That's our house!"

Most people didn't understand the deeper meaning behind his words. Remember the rental house? The floor plan we wanted if we could have afforded to buy a home? Well, Matt and his team built us that house. In a truly extreme way.

Our house. Those are sweet words to me. There were so many people from the show and from the community who came together to build *our house*. They studied, they researched, they learned. And what they built was incredible. I don't know how Matt did it, but that question he asked us the very first day? Well, he made sure we had a backup generator for the house. One that will run the air-conditioning and power to the house in case of an outage. Amazing. Josh's room was built with a castle for a bed and a 10-foot dragon reading chair based on the DragonKeeper series of his favorite author, Donita K. Paul. Kayla was given her underwater dream in her bedroom, including her wish for a waterbed.

The Extreme Team not only met our medical needs, but they also provided fun as well. We have a bowling alley in our basement. And 1964 Ford Mustangs. And a theater. And an ice-cream parlor. But we also have temperature sensors, purified water, an air-purification system, and tinted windows.

The tinted windows by Vista Window Film aren't noticeable to most people. But friends who were really close to us noticed right away. They walked in the house and gasped, saying, "Kim! Your blinds are open!"

All these years we've had to keep the blinds closed and cover the windows with heavy coverings to try and keep the heat out. It was an amazing feeling to open the blinds and know that the window film was protecting Kayla. She could now look out the windows when it was too hot for her to go outside. It was a beautiful thing.

The temperature sensors by ADT, along with the heating-and-cooling system by Bryant, made sure that the interior temperature wouldn't rise above where it needed to be. I didn't have to continually check Kayla's temperature inside anymore because the house helped me out.

The air purification by IQAir and the water treatment by Kerns provided new health for all of us, but especially for Josh and Kayla.

The homeschool room, bright and lively, was a place for the kids to look forward to spending many hours a day. All the bedrooms were safe havens of relaxation and joy. And the kitchen, with its beauty and functionality, was the central hub for all of us to talk about the day and enjoy one another's company. These things and more are examples of how a house can truly change your life. Our new home definitely gave us a new start—for health and to enjoy life.

Then, there's the new vehicle from Ford Motor Company. It's a beauty. Large enough to hold us and all the cooling gear, and with air-conditioned seats (the actual seats have A/C!) to help keep Kayla cool in the warm months. It's an amazing and wonderful feeling to know that we're safe traveling out in the heat. What an incredible gift from Ford.

Our community also gave us a fresh start with their fund-raising. The events that took place at Mr. Biggs while we were in Breckenridge raised enough money to pay off almost half of our medical bills. When Ty pulled Jeremy and me beside the bus to tell us the news, I wanted to sit on the ground and cry. Colorado Springs is an incredible place with incredible people, and those people gave of their time, energy, money, and hearts to help a family that most of them didn't know personally. It amazes me to this day.

Reflections

Many stories were shared with me in the days and weeks that followed Reveal Day. People would drive by and leave notes and pictures on the front porch. Hundreds of them. Reading all the thoughts and impressions of these different people gave me a small glimpse of how my family wasn't the only one touched by this experience.

"We were blessed in a magnificent way to be a part of this."

"Thank you for blessing *us* with this opportunity."

"You'll never know how my life was changed by participating in this week."

"This week turned my life completely around. Thank you."

"You don't know me, but you have changed my life with your story. I will never be the same again. Thank you so very much for inspiring us all."

I called our builder, Matt, to read him some of the notes and share the incredibly uplifting stories. He told me something I'll never forget: "Kim, I believe there are people who benefited even more than you did from being a part of this experience." Those words shocked me, and he's shared them with me many times since then as a gentle reminder. I felt so overwhelmingly blessed by the whole experience, how could I understand that Matt's words were true? And yet they were. We were given a home and a second chance, with physical needs being met. Other people received more than material possessions—things personal, private, and sacred in their own lives. It's very humbling to see the entire picture and what small part we played.

My friend Lori was touched by the care of the crew. Ed, especially, had quite an effect with my children's friends, who were brought in to work on some projects for the schoolroom. Lori told me later, "Ed was amazing with the children. Upon entering, he instantly became this big kid who sat down with the children and started to color. All the while he was asking questions of the children about you, the Woodhouse family. The way he related to the task at hand said volumes about his character, and I knew for me, as a parent on the sidelines, I would always remember that."

It's true. The designers and crew affected so many people's lives. Those who didn't have the opportunity to work with them often asked me, "Are the designers really as nice as they seem on TV?"

My answer's simply this: yes.

It reminded me of a quote from Diane Korman, senior producer of *Extreme Makeover: Home Edition*:

> The crew on *Extreme Makeover: Home Edition* cares so much about all our families. This is not just a job to them, it's about helping people and making a difference in communities. They really are as nice as you see on TV. If they wanted an easy job, believe me, they would work somewhere else.

They really cared. Many people who worked for the show were asked during the week, "Why do you work for the show? There's not much free time, or downtime, and the days are really long." But every time, the answers were positive and given with a smile. They wanted to help people, they wanted to give back, they loved working with families and children, they wanted to be a part of something that was bigger than themselves. Getting a glimpse into these people's lives brought tears to my eyes and a smile to my heart. And I thought to myself, *We need more shows and people like this.*

Matt shared with me how extraordinary it was to have such vast numbers of people working, simultaneously and together. In my mind I imagined it looking like an anthill. Thousands of workers all moving in their assigned jobs.

For example, our mechanical room holds so many vital pieces of equipment that make our lives better every day. This 8-by-10-foot room held 20 to 25 people—all of them focused on their specific jobs, all working in complete cooperation with one another. Matt told me it still gives him a smile to think about it. All over the build site, people lent their tools to one another and offered extra sets of hands when the call came for help. They finished the house in 96 hours—72 hours short of seven days.

It truly was inspirational.

In his own words, Matt shared his feelings with me about reflecting on that incredible, extreme week:

> Ultimately, each person gave all they could. Nobody left until they were empty. For that, as the builder, I could not be prouder of the building community and the people of Colorado. The success of this weighs equally on each person who contributed. . . .
>
> Looking back on my life, I've drifted toward and pulled away from God and my internal beliefs. Each person should only be so lucky as I to be a part of something like this that eliminates all doubt. God exists, and He is good.

What a profound statement.

Life After Extreme Makeover: Home Edition

When a surprise like EMHE happens, you can't prepare for what will occur afterward. Thousands of people drove by our house to get a glimpse of it, and hundreds of people stopped by to leave notes, cards, gifts, or simply words of encouragement. The outpouring of love from people was truly amazing.

The kids were given scholarships to the University of Colorado at Colorado Springs, our family was given a trip to the 2008 U.S. Olympic Team Trials by USA Swimming, and many, many other wonderful things.

When the *Extreme Makeover: Home Edition* show aired, I heard for the first time some of the designers' heartfelt comments. Ty said, "This . . . is about sacrifice. It's about a family that's given up everything they had, including their home, to keep their daughter alive." And, "They never gave up on hope."

After their intense research into our story, Ty, Ed, Tanya, Eduardo, and Rib all understood firsthand what this home meant to us. Ed said, "They do spend most of their life inside their house." And Ty said, "A home is more important than ever because it's more than just a place to live; it's a sanctuary—it's the only safe place that you have."[2]

I was once again amazed at the team from *Extreme Makeover* and all they sacrificed for our family.

The Montel Williams Show called again and asked us to make an appearance on an episode titled "Miraculous Kids." They had no idea we'd been chosen by EMHE when they called, but they were pleased to add that wonderful event to the story. The producers from Montel found out about Kayla's love for David Phelps and how he traveled to Colorado for the benefit during the build. They also knew that Kayla had never met David and that it was a dream of hers. So they planned a wonderful surprise for our daughter, and at the end of the show, out walked David carrying a bouquet of flowers. He told Kayla he was there to spend the day with her in New York City. Kayla's face lit up, and it melted my heart to see her wish granted.

During our trip to New York, David and his manager, Jim Chaffee, offered another special treat for our family. They invited us to attend David's taping of his new Christmas DVDs. Kayla wanted to go so badly, as did the rest of us, but we were worried about the temperature issues. You see, David would be filming in his beautifully renovated barn, but there was no air-conditioning, hundreds of people would be there, and we couldn't predict the weather.

Again I shouldn't ever be surprised at God's handiwork, because wouldn't you know, He brought a cold front through. It was cold in the barn that night, and we had the time of our lives.

David and his wife, Lori, welcomed us with open arms and made us feel like family. Their genuine love, care, and generosity has touched our family time and again. There will always be a special bond between us.

The evening was beyond anything we could have imagined. The first concert was filmed, and that Christmas DVD titled *O Holy Night* released in the fall of 2008. David sang everything with gusto and from his heart. It was the best musical performance I'd ever seen. I clapped and smiled and floated on cloud nine the whole time, watching my sweet children soak up the love and joy that filled the venue. I didn't think it could get any better. And then . . . the second concert began.

David shared with the audience that night that God was so cool because He provided the perfect weather for our family to be able to attend. There were some ladies sitting behind us who had been quite cold as the night began, and I felt so awful hearing their discomfort. But when David spoke about our incredible journey and our ability to attend because of the cold weather, the crowd stood and applauded. I, of course, cried. A lot.

David smiled straight at Kayla several times, and I don't think her face could have beamed her joy any brighter. Attending a David Phelps concert was her dream, and it had just come true. But the night wasn't over. At one point during that incredible second concert, David began to walk off the stage. (I don't think the camera crews knew what he was up to because all of a sudden they scurried around trying to follow him.) Before I realized his intent, he was standing in front of Kayla, reaching for her hand to help her stand, and then sweetly touching her face as he sang. It was probably the most precious moment I'd witnessed in my little girl's life. The moment felt surreal as the sea of people began to stand and applaud with everything in them. We all know what an outstanding musician David is, but seeing his tender heart on top of that was enough to lift the rafters. My eyes were filled with tears, and my heart overflowed with incredible thanksgiving for this amazing man and what he'd just done for Kayla.

At the conclusion of the night, I was still in shock from all that had taken place—David offering the chance to attend, God providing the weather, the warm welcome of all the "Phelps Phans," the joyous music celebrating the birth of our Savior, and David's special moment with my daughter. Several people stopped me afterward and said they didn't think there was a "dry eye in the house" when David sang to Kayla. And when that Christmas DVD releases in the fall of 2009, with the special part David did with Kayla, I don't think there will be many people who know about our story who will have dry eyes watching it. You know I'll be one of the first ones to purchase it and relive one of the most breathtaking and beautiful nights of my life.

There were other TV shows that contacted us, as well as newspapers and magazines. The Discovery Health Channel filmed an episode based on our story titled "Painful Truth" for their show *Mystery ER*. And many other articles were done across the country.

Southern Living at Home donated tons of beautiful items for our house during EMHE and called to check on us several months later. It had thrilled me to have their products because *Southern Living* had always been a favorite magazine of mine. But even more than that, all the pieces looked as if they had been specifically designed for my home, with my own personal tastes in mind.

Gary Wright of Southern Living at Home invited me to speak for their national convention. A team flew out to film a beautiful video for their conference, and in June they brought our whole family out to Nashville. Our little trip was extraordinary. They took care of us and all our needs. Every little detail was paid attention to, and we were treated like kings and queens. Southern Living at Home knows how to create that homelike atmosphere no matter where you are, and we had a ball.

Later that month the kids, Holly, my sister (Mary), and I traveled to Omaha, Nebraska, for the U.S. Olympic Swim Team Trials. Amazing doesn't even begin to describe that experience. World records were broken several times over, and the U.S. swimmers were incredible. It was a thrill just getting a glimpse at this step in what the athletes had been working for. And at the trials, Kayla and Josh were inspired to take their swimming to the next level.

Returning home we spent a lot of time researching swim teams, and the wonderful folks at USA Swimming helped. When we found Cheyenne Mountain Aquatics, I called head coach Joe Novak and spoke with him about Josh and Kayla. We didn't want any special treatment, but Jeremy and I did want a place the kids would be comfortable, where they would work hard, would learn a lot, and the coaches would understand about Kayla's special needs.

Coach Novak was of the highest integrity, and his team of coaches and swimmers impressed me. We'd found the right one.

Today

So where are we today?

We are in our Extreme Home, loving every minute of it. We homeschool, I write, and we spend about five hours every day, six days a week, between two different swimming pools. We are blessed.

Kayla's health has skyrocketed. Her temperature issues have been gradually getting better; in fact, the thermostat in the house is all the way up to 64 degrees now—woo hoo! Her skin is almost completely healed, and the neurosurgeon has totally cleared her. She doesn't have to go back!

Josh has also had extreme health improvements. Ever since his battle as a child with croup, Josh suffered from asthma. But in the time we've been in our new home, he hasn't had one asthma attack. Amazing.

Even with all the publicity, the thousands of people who e-mail through the Web site and the re-airing of shows we've been on, we're still "normal." At least according to *my* definition.

With all the blessings, there are still tough times. A few people were upset with inaccuracies in the TV shows. Our story is complicated, and it's hard to get everything exactly perfect. Our own family has a hard time getting the details straight, but when those inaccuracies involved other people, it hurt them. And there has been so much contact from around the world that we've tried to help as many people as we can, even if it's just encouragement. But on the flip side of that, it has taken time away from good friends. And I miss them.

There was even a point right after the build when the world seemed to come crashing in again. I felt as if the Enemy was constantly trying to attack and steal our joy. But we didn't let that happen. I stomped out onto my porch one day with a flag, which said, "Praise God from Whom All Blessings Flow." As I hung it up on the flagpole, with gritted teeth I said, "My joy will not be taken away. I am going to praise God. I am going to consider it pure joy!" I stomped my foot again in emphasis, showing my determination not to get discouraged. I would not forget that incredible blessings sometimes come with incredible trials.

We do a lot more traveling now as I speak and share the story with others. And we're very thankful for the health improvements that have made this possible. It also helps that millions of people have seen us on one show or another, and there's so much understanding and help everywhere we go.

And we'll never be able to thank each person who gave of themselves to bless us during *Extreme Makeover*. Close friends who stayed at the site day and night, making certain everyone really understood Kayla's needs. Friends who spent hours on phone calls and in face-to-face conversations with everyone who had questions. Friends who contacted stores and organizations for donations. As well as complete strangers who heard about the need and rose to the challenge.

Every morning I wake up and look around. I think about all the people it took to make this possible, and I'm so very grateful. I'm sure it wasn't easy, and it took great sacrifice.

Pure Joy

Life is hard, but God is good. Our lives haven't been easy. And I'm just guessing here, but yours hasn't been a piece of cake either, has it?

How do *you* face the day-to-day trials? Have you figured out how to find the joy?

Through the journey of our story, I pray that you have been blessed and seen that even in the hardest circumstances, God is there. Even when the world seems to be crashing in, God is joy. And no matter what, you *can* keep going.

Many things can hinder your joy. One of them is sin. Sin dents your joy. Let me give you an illustration to remember this point. I always wear sunglasses on top of my head. One reason is that my eyes are really sensitive, and I need them even when it's raining. Another reason is that I have a lot of hair, and they help keep it off my face. And, of course, the quintessential reason is so that I won't forget them. Anyway, about a year ago Katelyn, who does our hair, noticed that I have a dent on the top of my head. (Anyone guess where this is headed?) She proclaimed, "Wow! You've got quite a dent in your head." And then, as if the lightbulb had suddenly come to life and shone brightly, she laughed. "It's from your sunglasses!"

Of course, I was sitting in the chair with my head in a shampoo bowl rolling my eyes at her, until I reached up and felt the dent. It was really there. Not only did *I* feel it, but several other people came over to check out my dent.

The point to my little story here is that I have a permanent dent in my scalp from wearing my sunglasses on top of my head for 20-plus years. It's the same with sin. When we allow the same sin to continue in our lives, it dents our joy. We can't have the same unfathomable, amazing, exciting, bask-in-His-glory joy when we continue in sin. Our fellowship is hindered by sin, and we distance ourselves from that life-changing relationship.

Wow. Ouch, that hurts.

Another stealer of our joy is when we wallow in self-pity, in lack of self-confidence, in the crises of our daily lives. It's so easy to wallow, and sometimes even comforting, at least for a little while.

When I begin to wallow, I recite James 1:2–4. Sometimes I don't want to, but I do it anyway. There's something about putting on a positive attitude that makes you want to cringe at these times, but as soon as you've done it, your perspective will be clear again.

Wallowing is the reason I came up with our five-cent fine. There is no whining, grumbling, or complaining in our house—or you pay the fine. It's a great way to stop the wallow before it starts and another way to remind yourself about looking at the positive rather than the negative.

Rejoice. Be thankful. Don't compare your life with anyone else's.

So what if you're not like someone else? Everybody's spiritual race is different, with unusual circumstances and distinctive events. Your race is unlike mine. My race is unlike yours. Learning how to grab on to God's joy has made running the distance easier for me, and it will for you as well.

The more I consider it joy, the closer I grow to Him as I make my way toward that mature-and-complete finish line.

There will still be massive hurdles, potholes, mud puddles, and speed bumps along the way. But I will continue to say, "Consider it pure joy," as I cling to the Master, and He reminds me to "keep going, don't quit."

Joy.

My life is full of joy.

Resources

David Phelps, www.davidphelps.com—David's official Web site.

Gift of Pain, www.gift-of-pain.org—The Gingras family started this foundation to help other children with the rare nerve disorder Kayla and Gabby both have.

Heat Relief Depot, www.heatreliefdepot.com—An extensive site that has an abundant supply of useful equipment for heating and cooling. Kayla's cooling vests and equipment all came from the Heat Relief Depot. Mention Kim Woodhouse or Kayla Woodhouse when you contact them. Phone: 1-877-879-1450

Kimberley Woodhouse, www.kimberleywoodhouse.com—Check out Kim's Web site to learn about other upcoming releases and to contact her.

Precept Ministries, www.precept.org—Precept Ministries' Web site offers a wealth of Bible studies and study aids. The Woodhouse family uses them extensively.

Notes

Chapter 2

1. Cyberspace Association of U.S. Submariners, "HED Foundation and CAUSS," http://www.subnet.com/hed/hednew.htm (address no longer active).

Chapter 5

1. Mandi Maxwell, " 'KoolVest' Girl, Family Move to Alaska for More Normal Life," *Town Talk*, June 23, 2001.
2. Kimberley Woodhouse, "You Are," copyright © 2002. All rights reserved.

Chapter 6

1. Kimberley Woodhouse, "You'll Always Be There," copyright © 2002. All rights reserved.
2. Elizabeth George, *A Woman After God's Own Heart* (Eugene, OR: Harvest House, 1997), 24–29.

Chapter 8

1. Charles R. Swindoll, *Three Steps Forward, Two Steps Back: Persevering Through Pressure*, rev. ed. (Nashville: Word Publishing, 1997), 83.
2. Kimberley Woodhouse, "Hallelujah," copyright © 2002. All rights reserved.
3. Andrew Stanton, David Reynolds, and Bob Peterson, "Just Keep Swimming," *Finding Nemo* (Pixar Films, 2003).

Chapter 9

1. Charles R. Swindoll, *The Finishing Touch: Becoming God's Masterpiece* (Dallas: Word Publishing, 1994), 8.

Chapter 10

1. Andrea Brown, "It's Not So Easy Being a Superhero," *Gazette*, May 20, 2006.

2. Kay Arthur, *His Imprint, My Expression: Changed Forever by the Master's Touch* (Eugene, OR: Harvest House, 1993), 77–79.

Chapter 12

1. Andrew Wineke, "One Cool Makeover," *Gazette*, October 8, 2007.

2. Ty Pennington and Ed Sanders, interviews in *Extreme Makeover: Home Edition*, ABC, January 13, 2008.

FOCUS ON THE FAMILY®

Welcome to the Family

Whether you purchased this book, borrowed it, or received it as a gift, we're glad you're reading it. It's just one of the many helpful, encouraging, and biblically based resources produced by Focus on the Family® for people in all stages of life.

Focus began in 1977 with the vision of one man, Dr. James Dobson, a licensed psychologist and author of numerous best-selling books on marriage, parenting, and family. Alarmed by the societal, political, and economic pressures that were threatening the existence of the American family, Dr. Dobson founded Focus on the Family with one employee and a once-a-week radio broadcast aired on 36 stations.

Now an international organization reaching millions of people daily, Focus on the Family is dedicated to preserving values and strengthening and encouraging families through the life-changing message of Jesus Christ.

Focus on the Family MAGAZINES

These faith-building, character-developing publications address the interests, issues, concerns, and challenges faced by every member of your family from preschool through the senior years.

For More INFORMATION

ONLINE:
Log on to
FocusOnTheFamily.com
In Canada, log on to
FocusOnTheFamily.ca

PHONE:
Call toll-free:
800-A-FAMILY
(232-6459)
In Canada, call toll-free:
800-661-9800

FOCUS ON THE FAMILY® MAGAZINE	FOCUS ON THE FAMILY CLUBHOUSE JR.® Ages 4 to 8	FOCUS ON THE FAMILY CLUBHOUSE® Ages 8 to 12	FOCUS ON THE FAMILY CITIZEN® U.S. news issues

Rev. 12/08

More Great Resources
from Focus on the Family®

Experiencing God Around the Kitchen Table
By Marilynn Blackaby & Carrie Blackaby Webb
Pull up a chair and have a seat at the kitchen table of someone who has faced life's blessings and its trials. Marilynn Blackaby has often been asked about the challenges of raising five children while her husband, Henry, was heavily involved in ministry and frequently away from home. With grace and humor, Marilynn weaves in lessons she's learned over the years as she shares her personal stories. Marilynn's experiences and wisdom will bring hope and encouragement to your heart.

Gone in a Heartbeat
Our Daughters Died… Our Faith Endures
Inside the New Life Church shootings
By David & Marie Works with Dean Merrill
The shootings at New Life Church are one of America's greatest recent tragedies. At the heart of that tragedy is the Works family. A mom and dad left to cope without two of their daughters, two sisters left to grieve the loss of their siblings. For the first time, David and Marie Works reveal the complete story of that fateful day, how they've coped since then, details of their emotional meeting with the gunman's family, and what they learned when a parent's worst nightmare became reality. For anyone facing their world turned upside down, *Gone in a Heartbeat* tells a true story of hope and fearless faith.

Light from Lucas: Lessons in Faith from a Fragile Life
By Bob Vander Plaats
The third of four children, Lucas was severely disabled at birth. Through the silent instruction of Lucas, the author and his family relates dozens of lessons they've learned—from knowing God and discovering the value of every life, to practical ideas on parenting and why we suffer.

FOR MORE INFORMATION

 Online:
Log on to FocusOnTheFamily.com
In Canada, log on to focusonthefamily.ca.

 Phone:
Call toll free: 800-A-FAMILY
In Canada, call toll free: 800-661-9800.

BPZZXP1

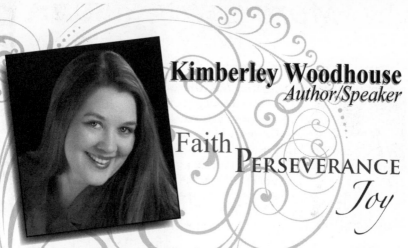

Kimberley Woodhouse
Author/Speaker

Faith **PERSEVERANCE** *Joy*

Kimberley Woodhouse and her family were introduced to millions of TV viewers when they were featured on ABC's hit program *Extreme Makeover: Home Edition*. This followed years of front-page newspaper stories, national magazines articles, and medical journals. Since the ABC show aired, they have shared their story on *The Montel Williams Show*, Discovery Health Channel's *Mystery ER*, and hundreds of other media appearances.

A popular speaker, Kim has shared her quick wit, enthusiasm, and positive outlook through difficult circumstances in person, speaking to more than 600 churches, conferences, retreats, and seminars across the country.

As a third generation Liszt student, she has passed down her love of the arts to hundreds of students over the years and recorded three music albums.

She is a member of ACFW (American Christian Fiction Writers), the Vice President of the Colorado Springs Chapter, and active on the Colorado Area Board for ACFW. In addition to her non-fiction writing, she writes romantic suspense and children's books.

Kimberley lives, writes, and homeschools in Colorado with her husband and two children in their truly "extreme" home.

Find Kim online at www.kimberleywoodhouse.com, Facebook, and Twitter.com/kimwoodhouse.